System Administration NetWare® 3.12

This training manual may be used:

- for the System Administration NetWare 3.12 course.

- as a study guide for Novell course 508, Administration 3.12, test # 50-130.

- as a study guide for Certified Novell Administrator (CNA) test # 50-390, NetWare 3.12 Administration.

- as a NetWare reference manual.

© 1993 - 95 · PC Age, Inc. All Rights Reserved · 20 Audrey Place · Fairfield, NJ 07004 · U.S.A. · Tel: 201-882-5370

Copyright © 1993-95 by PC Age, Inc. All rights reserved. No part of this work may be reproduced or transmitted in any form or by any means, electronic or mechanical, including photocopying or recording, or by any information storage or retrieval system without the prior written permission of PC Age, Inc., unless such copying is expressly permitted by federal copyright law. Address inquiries to PC Age, Inc., 20 Audrey Place; Fairfield, NJ 07004, U.S.A.

This book is sold as is, without warranty of any kind, either express or implied, respecting the contents of this book, including but not limited to implied warranties for the book's quality, performance, merchantability, or fitness for any particular purpose. Neither PC Age, Inc., nor its resellers shall be liable to the purchaser or any other person or entity with respect to any liability, loss, or damage caused or alleged to be caused directly or indirectly by this book. Further, PC Age, Inc. reserves the right to make changes to any and all parts of this manual at any time, without obligation to notify any person or entity of such changes.

ISBN 1-57739-001-6

PC Age guarantees that if the Novell certification test based on this manual changes within 6 weeks from the purchased date of the course manual, PC Age will replace the manual with the updated one free of charge. Please arrange to take the Novell test within the six week period. In the United States and Canada, call 1-800-RED-EXAM (1-800-733-3926) to arrange the Novell test.

Contents

CHAPTER 1: NETWARE BASICS

NETWORKING BASICS 1-1
   NETWORK 1-1
   SERVER 1-1
   CLIENT 1-2
DISTRIBUTED PROCESSING 1-2
CENTRAL PROCESSING 1-2
WORKSTATION ENVIRONMENTS SUPPORTED BY NETWARE 3.12 1-3
REVIEW QUESTIONS 1-4

CHAPTER 2: SYSTEM FAULT TOLERANCE

SYSTEM FAULT TOLERANT CAPABILITIES 2-1
   READ-AFTER-WRITE VERIFICATION 2-1
   DUPLICATE DETs AND FATs 2-1
   DISK MIRRORING AND DUPLEXING 2-2
   TRANSACTION TRACKING SYSTEM (TTS) 2-2
   UPS MONITORING 2-2
REVIEW QUESTIONS 2-3

CHAPTER 3: NETWARE 3.12 UTILITIES

WORKSTATION UTILITIES 3-1
COMMAND LINE UTILITIES 3-1
MENU UTILITIES 3-1
NETWARE GUI UTILITIES 3-2
USING USER TOOLS 3-4
USING ELECTROTEXT 3-7
FILE SERVER UTILITIES 3-9
   CONSOLE COMMANDS 3-9

© 1993 - 95 · PC Age, Inc. All Rights Reserved · 20 Audrey Place · Fairfield, NJ 07004 · U.S.A. · Tel: 201-882-5370

NETWARE LOADABLE MODULES (NLMS) 3-9
IMPORTANT MANAGEMENT NLM UTILITIES 3-10
   INSTALL 3-10
   MONITOR 3-10
   SOURCE ROUTING SUPPORT 3-11
   REMOTE BOOTING 3-11
REVIEW QUESTIONS 3-12

CHAPTER 4: DIRECTORY AND FILE MANAGEMENT

NETWARE DIRECTORY STRUCTURE 4-1
   NETWARE VOLUMES 4-1
NETWARE-CREATED DIRECTORIES 4-3
DIRECTORIES YOU SHOULD CREATE ON THE SERVER 4-5
   HOME DIRECTORIES 4-6
   APPLICATION DIRECTORY 4-7
   DOS DIRECTORIES 4-7
   SHARED DATA AREA 4-7
MULTIPLE VOLUME SERVER 4-8
   ADVANTAGES 4-8
   DISADVANTAGES 4-9
CREATING DIRECTORIES ON THE SERVER 4-10
   USING DOS TO CREATE DIRECTORIES 4-10
UTILITIES USED FOR VIEWING SERVER INFORMATION 4-11
   SLIST 4-11
   USING THE NETWARE FILER UTILITY TO CREATE DIRECTORIES 4-11
   REMOVING A DIRECTORY USING THE FILER UTILITY 4-12
UTILITIES USED FOR VIEWING VOLUME INFORMATION 4-15
   VOLINFO 4-15
   CHKVOL 4-15
   FILER 4-15
UTILITIES USED TO VIEW OR CHANGE INFORMATION ABOUT DIRECTORIES ... 4-16
   LISTDIR 4-16
   NDIR 4-17
   FILES 4-17
   SUBDIRECTORIES 4-18
   DIRECTORIES 4-18
   CHKDIR 4-21
   DSPACE 4-21
   RENDIR 4-22
MANAGING FILES WITH THE FILER UTILITY 4-24
COPYING DIRECTORIES AND FILES USING THE NCOPY COMMAND 4-24

© 1993 - 95 · PC Age, Inc. All Rights Reserved · 20 Audrey Place · Fairfield, NJ 07004 · U.S.A. · Tel: 201-882-5370

MANAGING DELETED FILES WITH SALVAGE AND PURGE 4-25
    SALVAGE 4-25
    PURGE 4-25
REVIEW QUESTIONS 4-26
HANDS-ON EXERCISES 4-28
    UNDERSTANDING LOGGING IN 4-28
    UNDERSTANDING THE DIRECTORY STRUCTURE 4-28
    USING THE DSPACE UTILITY 4-29
    USING THE SALVAGE UTILITY 4-29

CHAPTER 5: DRIVE MAPPINGS

DRIVE MAPPINGS 5-1
    NETWORK DRIVES 5-1
    NETWORK DRIVE MAPPING 5-3
    SEARCH DRIVES 5-5
    SEARCH DRIVE MAPPING 5-5
    SEARCH MAPPINGS AND THE DOS PATH ENVIRONMENT 5-6
DELETING A MAPPING 5-8
REVIEW QUESTIONS 5-9
HANDS-ON EXERCISE 5-12
    UNDERSTANDING DRIVE MAPPINGS 5-12

CHAPTER 6: SETTING UP USERS AND GROUPS

USERS 6-1
GROUPS 6-1
DISTRIBUTED NETWORK MANAGEMENT 6-2
    WORKGROUP MANAGER 6-2
    WHAT WORKGROUP MANAGERS CAN DO 6-2
    WHAT WORKGROUP MANAGERS CAN'T DO 6-2
USER ACCOUNT MANAGER 6-3
    WHAT USER ACCOUNT MANAGERS CAN DO 6-3
    WHAT USER ACCOUNT MANAGERS CAN'T DO 6-3
CONSOLE OPERATOR 6-3
UTILITIES FOR CREATING USERS AND GROUPS 6-5
    THE SYSCON UTILITY 6-5
MAKEUSER AND USERDEF 6-11
    MAKEUSER 6-11
    MAKEUSER KEYWORDS 6-12

USERDEF	6-21
REVIEW QUESTIONS	6-23

CHAPTER 7: SECURITY

SECURITY LEVELS	7-1
LOGIN/PASSWORD RESTRICTIONS	7-1
STATION, TIME, AND OTHER ACCOUNT RESTRICTIONS	7-2
RIGHTS SECURITY	7-3
NETWARE 3.12 RIGHTS	7-4
RIGHTS REQUIREMENTS	7-6
TRUSTEE RIGHTS ASSIGNMENTS	7-7
THE INHERITED RIGHTS MASK (IRM)	7-7
EFFECTIVE RIGHTS	7-8
EXERCISE 7.1	7-11
ATTRIBUTE SECURITY	7-11
FILE AND DIRECTORY ATTRIBUTES	7-12
OTHER ATTRIBUTES	7-15
FILE SERVER SECURITY	7-16
THE NETWARE BINDERY	7-17
USING SECURITY-RELATED NETWARE COMMANDS	7-18
ALLOW	7-18
GRANT	7-18
REVOKE	7-18
REMOVE	7-19
FLAG	7-19
FLAGDIR	7-19
TLIST	7-20
RIGHTS	7-20
NCP PACKET SIGNATURE	7-20
SERVER LEVELS	7-21
WORKSTATION LEVELS	7-22
EFFECTIVE PACKET SIGNATURE OF SERVER AND WORKSTATION	7-23
ANSWER TO EXERCISE 7.1	7-24
REVIEW QUESTIONS	7-25

CHAPTER 8: MANAGING THE WORKSTATION CONNECTION

CONNECTING A WORKSTATION	8-1
NETWARE DOS REQUESTER	8-1
COMMUNICATION PROTOCOL	8-2

OPEN DATA-LINK INTERFACE (ODI)	8-3
SOFTWARE TO CONNECT A DOS WORKSTATION	8-5
WORKSTATION CONFIGURATION FILES	8-7
CONFIG.SYS	8-7
AUTOEXEC.BAT	8-7
NET.CFG	8-8
SUPPORTING WINDOWS WORKSTATIONS	8-9
INSTALLING WORKSTATION SOFTWARE	8-9
REVIEW QUESTIONS	8-10

CHAPTER 9: LOGIN SCRIPTS

TYPES OF LOGIN SCRIPTS	9-1
SYSTEM LOGIN SCRIPT	9-1
USER LOGIN SCRIPT	9-2
DEFAULT LOGIN SCRIPT	9-2
LOGIN SCRIPT COMMANDS	9-2
#	9-2
ATTACH	9-3
BREAK ON/OFF	9-4
COMSPEC	9-4
DISPLAY	9-4
DOS BREAK ON/OFF	9-5
DOS SET	9-5
DOS VERIFY ON/OFF	9-5
DRIVE	9-5
EXIT	9-6
FDISPLAY	9-6
FIRE PHASERS	9-7
GOTO	9-7
IF...THEN...ELSE	9-8
INCLUDE	9-9
MACHINE	9-9
MAP	9-9
NO_DEFAULT	9-10
PAUSE	9-10
PCCOMPATIBLE	9-10
REMARK	9-11
SHIFT	9-11
WRITE	9-12
SAMPLE SYSTEM AND USER LOGIN SCRIPTS	9-14
SYSTEM LOGIN SCRIPT	9-14

System Administration NetWare 3.12

    USER LOGIN SCRIPT 9-15
    REVIEW QUESTIONS 9-16

CHAPTER 10: NETWARE MENUS

    OVERVIEW 10-1
    PREPARING A MENU 10-1
    A SIMPLE SAMPLE MENU 10-2
    SOURCE COMMANDS 10-2
        ORGANIZATIONAL COMMANDS 10-2
        CONTROL COMMANDS 10-4
    COMPILING MENUS 10-9
    EXECUTING MENUS 10-9
    COMPATIBILITY WITH EARLIER VERSIONS 10-10
    REVIEW QUESTIONS 10-12

CHAPTER 11: INSTALLING APPLICATIONS

    INSTALLING APPLICATIONS ON A NETWORK 11-1
    REVIEW QUESTIONS 11-3

CHAPTER 12: BACKUP

    OVERVIEW 12-1
    STRATEGIES FOR BACKUP AND RESTORE 12-1
        INCREMENTAL BACKUP 12-2
        DIFFERENTIAL BACKUP 12-2
    RESTORE STRATEGIES 12-2
    BACKUP RESPONSIBILITIES 12-3
    NOVELL SUPPLIED SERVICES 12-3
        SBACKUP PROCESS 12-4
    REVIEW QUESTIONS 12-6

CHAPTER 13: PRINTING

    PRINTING ON A NETWORK 13-1
    NETWARE PRINT SERVER 13-1
    REMOTE PRINTER SOFTWARE 13-2

© 1993 - 95 · PC Age, Inc. All Rights Reserved · 20 Audrey Place · Fairfield, NJ 07004 · U.S.A. · Tel: 201-882-5370

PCONSOLE	13-3
NETWORK PRINTING STEPS	13-4
CREATING QUEUES	13-4
CREATING A PRINT SERVER ACCOUNT AND DEFINING PRINTERS	13-4
ASSIGNING PRINT QUEUES TO PRINTERS	13-5
LOADING THE PRINT SERVER PROGRAM	13-6
RUNNING RPRINTER	13-7
THE CAPTURE COMMAND	13-11
CAPTURE OPTIONS	13-11
ENDING THE CAPTURE COMMAND	13-12
ALL	13-13
CANCEL	13-13
CANCELALL	13-13
CANCELLOCAL=N	13-13
LOCAL=N	13-13
NETWORK PRINTING FROM MS WINDOWS	13-14
THE NPRINT COMMAND	13-14
NPRINT OPTIONS	13-14
SPOOL (CONSOLE COMMAND)	13-16
PRINTDEF	13-17
PRINTCON	13-17
NETWORK PRINTING USERS	13-18
REVIEW QUESTIONS	13-19

CHAPTER 14: REMOTE MANAGEMENT

REMOTE CONSOLE OPERATOR	14-2
NETWARE SUPERVISOR	14-2
USING REMOTE MANAGEMENT	14-2
FILE SERVER SOFTWARE FOR REMOTE MANAGEMENT	14-3
REMOTE.NLM	14-3
RSPX.NLM	14-3
RS232.NLM	14-3
WORKSTATION SOFTWARE FOR REMOTE MANAGEMENT	14-4
ACONSOLE.EXE	14-4
RCONSOLE.EXE	14-4
COMMUNICATION LINK TYPES	14-5
DIRECT LINK	14-5
ASYNCHRONOUS LINK	14-5
REDUNDANT LINK	14-5
SETTING UP REMOTE MANAGEMENT	14-6
HARDWARE AND SOFTWARE REQUIREMENTS	14-6

© 1993 - 95 · PC Age, Inc. All Rights Reserved · 20 Audrey Place · Fairfield, NJ 07004 · U.S.A. · Tel: 201-882-5370

    FILE SERVER REQUIREMENTS 14-6
    WORKSTATION REQUIREMENTS... 14-6
USING DIRECT LINK REMOTE MANAGEMENT 14-7
RCONSOLE MENU OPTIONS 14-9
    SELECT SCREEN... 14-9
    DIRECTORY SCAN 14-9
    COPY SYSTEM AND PUBLIC FILES 14-10
    SHELL TO OPERATING SYSTEM 14-10
    END REMOTE SESSION WITH SERVER (SHIFT-ESC) 14-10
    RESUME REMOTE SESSION WITH SERVER... 14-10
REBOOT A FILE SERVER FROM A REMOTE CONSOLE 14-11
REVIEW QUESTIONS 14-12

CHAPTER 15: ELECTRONIC MAIL

OVERVIEW 15-1
    BASIC MHS 15-1
    MAINTENANCE AND ADMINISTRATION.. 15-3
    USAGE 15-4
EXERCISES... 15-5
    ADMINISTRATION 15-5
    USAGE 15-5
REVIEW QUESTIONS 15-7

FINAL HANDS-ON EXERCISE
APPENDIX A
APPENDIX B
MULTIPLE-CHOICE PRACTICE QUESTIONS
ANSWERS TO REVIEW QUESTIONS
INDEX

Chapter 1   NetWare Basics

Networking Basics

Network

A network connects computers and peripherals so that they can communicate and share resources and data.

Server

A Server is a combination of hardware and software that manages the shared resources and provides services to other devices (clients) on the network. In a Novell Network, a computer with the NetWare operating system is a server.

There may be many types of servers in a network, but each network must have at least one File Server.

The file server stores all of the network's shared files, manages the shared hard drive(s), and makes sure that multiple requests— especially write requests— do not conflict with each other. To protect the data and prevent unauthorized access, the file server also maintains lists of rights and authorizations associated with the data files.

System Administration NetWare 3.12

Other servers on a **LAN** (Local Area Network) may be Communication Servers to manage communications, or Print Servers to manage printing, etc.

Client

Any device that requests services from a server is called a Client. A client may be a workstation, a printer, or another server.

The most common client on a network is the workstation.

Workstations on a LAN are personal computers. LANs do not support "dumb" terminals, like the type used in mini or mainframe environments.

NetWare workstations may be IBM PCs or compatibles, IBM PS/2s, Apple Macintoshes, or UNIX-based computers.

Distributed Processing

In a network environment, each workstation executes its own application(s). When a user runs any application stored on the server, the application and file or data are copied to the workstation's memory and processed there. This is called **Distributed Processing.**

Central Processing

In a mainframe or minicomputer system all processing is done on the main computer. This is called **Central Processing**. A mainframe or minicomputer supports dumb terminals that have limited or no processing power.

Workstation Environments Supported by NetWare 3.12

- DOS, OS/2, and Windows

- Macintosh workstations are supported through the optional NetWare for Macintosh 3.0 product and associated NLMs (NetWare Loadable Modules) that support the AFP (AppleTalk Filing Protocol).

  A five user support for Macintosh workstations is bundled with NetWare 3.12.

- UNIX workstations are supported by the optional NetWare NFS (Network File System) product and associated NLMs that support the NFS protocol.

- OSI (Open System Interconnection):
  NetWare 3.12 supports the OSI GOSIP (Government Open System Interconnection Profile) through the optional NetWare FTAM (File Transfer Access and Management) product.

Review Questions

Q.1. What is the most important reason for computer networking?

    a. sharing information   b. sharing resources

    c. sharing computers   d. sharing applications

Q.2. Every network must have a server called a _____ .

    a. server   b. file server

    c. print server   d. communication server

Q.3. A server can also be a client.

    a. true   b. false

Q.4. Which of the following is not supported by NetWare as a client?

    a. OS/2   b. Macintosh

    c. UNIX   d. NFS

Q.5. Name Space Support FTAM is provided as an optional product for which system?

a. Macintosh   b. UNIX

c. OSI   d. OS2

Chapter 2   System Fault Tolerance

System Fault Tolerant Capabilities

NetWare has two levels of **System Fault Tolerant (SFT)** features which provide protection from file and data loss and data mismatching. SFT I features Read-After-Write verification, Duplicate DETs (Directory Entry Tables) and FATs (File Allocation Tables), and the Hot Fix area. SFT II features Disk Mirroring, Disk Duplexing, TTS (Transaction Tracking System) and UPS (Uninterruptable Power Supply) monitoring. A description of these features follows:

Read-After-Write Verification

This feature verifies that the data written to the hard disk matches the original data still in memory. If there is a mismatch the OS assumes it has found a bad block, redirects the data to the predefined **Hot Fix** area, and marks the bad block unusable.

Duplicate DETs and FATs

NetWare uses DETs and FATs to keep track of files' information (file name, owner, date and time of last update, location, etc.). NetWare stores duplicate DETs and FATs on two separate areas of the hard disk. Therefore, if one set becomes corrupted, it reads information from the other set.

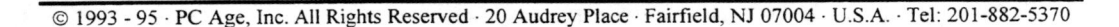

© 1993 - 95 · PC Age, Inc. All Rights Reserved · 20 Audrey Place · Fairfield, NJ 07004 · U.S.A. · Tel: 201-882-5370

Disk Mirroring and Duplexing

Disk Mirroring stores duplicate data on two hard disks connected to the same disk channel. Both hard disks must be the same logical size. If one disk fails, the OS automatically uses the other (mirrored) disk.

Disk Duplexing is the same as disk mirroring, but it also duplicates the disk coprocessor board (DCB), cable unit, and drive controller.

We set up disk mirroring or disk duplexing in the INSTALL.NLM utility.

Transaction Tracking System (TTS)

TTS protects database files from corruption by backing out incomplete transactions that result from a failure in network components or from a power failure. NetWare database files (bindery files, for example) are automatically protected by TTS. To protect files by TTS, you must set the "T" flag for your files because NetWare does not use transaction tracking on every file. Your application must also support NetWare TTS. Word processing documents are not protected by TTS.

UPS Monitoring

UPS Monitoring allows the file server to monitor an attached **Uninterruptible Power Supply**. When a power failure occurs, NetWare notifies all current users, closes any open files, and shuts itself down. To use UPS monitoring, you load UPS.NLM and then enter any parameters desired.

Note: Novell new SFT III provides servers mirroring.

Review Questions

Q.1. Which is not supported by TTS?

    a. database files   b. NetWare bindery files

    (c.) word processing files   d. NetWare database files

Q.2. Disk duplexing means _____ .

    (a.) separate disks   **(b.) separate controllers**

    (c.) separate disk channels   **(d.) separate cables**

Q.3. The NetWare utility used to activate mirroring/duplexing is called _____ .

    a. MIRROR.NLM   **(b.) INSTALL.NLM**

    c. INSTALL.EXE   d. MONITOR.NLM

Chapter 3 NetWare 3.12 Utilities

NetWare 3.12 provides the following types of utilities for network access, usage, and management:

- Workstation Utilities
- File server Utilities

Workstation Utilities

Workstation utilities are executed from the workstation. In NetWare we have command line utilities, menu utilities, and Graphical User Interface (GUI) utilities.

Command Line Utilities

These are commands you execute from the system prompt. For example: NDIR, MAP, LISTDIR.

Menu Utilities

Menu utilities are NetWare based-DOS or Text utilities that provide menus to select further options. For example, SYSCON, FILER, and DSPACE.

Menu Function Keys

The following keys can be used within NetWare Menu Utilities:

Keystroke(s)	Action(s)
RETURN	Selects or moves to the next level.
ESCAPE	Returns to previous level or exits.
INSERT	Adds an entry.
DELETE	Removes an entry.
F1	Provides help.
F1 F1	Defines function keys.
F3	Modifies.
F5	Marks multiple options (toggle switch).
ALT F10	Quickly exits without saving.
F10	Selects

NetWare GUI Utilities

NetWare 3.12 provides two GUI utilities:

- **NetWare User Tools:** This Windows utility provides a graphical interface to access network resources. NetWare User Tools let you manage drive mappings, printer connections and setup, server connections, and directory and file properties. You can also send and receive messages, etc.

- **ElectroText:** This Windows utility provides an electronic version of the NetWare manuals. We can choose a manual, browse its contents, search for a particular topic, and print the contents. For more information, see the "Using Novell ElectroText" section in the NetWare 3.12 *System Administration* manual.

These utilities are accessed from MS Windows and function like other MS Windows applications. You can press <F1> or select the Help menu option to get indexed and contextual help.

Using User Tools

1. Click on the **User Tools** icon from the Windows menu.

2. You will see different buttons on the top. The left most button (the one that shows a door) is used to exit from User Tools. You can exit User Tools by clicking with the mouse or by pressing **<Alt><X>**.

3. The next button (the one that shows two drives) is used to get information about **Drive Connections**. This button can be activated by clicking with the mouse or by pressing **<Alt><D>**. This option shows three boxes: Path, Drives, and Resources. The "Drives" box shows all the available drives and their mappings. You can see four buttons at the bottom: Drive Info, Permanent, Map Delete, and Map. Drive Info provides file server name, path, user's name, effective rights for current directory, etc. Permanent is used to make a drive mapping permanent. Delete Map is used to delete a drive mapping. Map is used for drive mapping.

4. The next button (the one that shows a printer) is used to get information about **Printer Connections**. This button can be activated by clicking with the mouse or by pressing **<Alt><P>**. This option shows three boxes: Queue, Ports, and Resources. The "Ports" box shows all the available ports. You can see four buttons at the bottom: LPT Settings, Permanent, End Capture, and Capture.

5. The next button (the one that shows a computer) is used to get information about **NetWare Connections**. This button can be activated by clicking with the mouse or by pressing

<Alt><C>. This option shows three boxes: Context, Connections, and Resources. You can see four buttons at the bottom: NetWare Info., Set Pass, Logout, and Login. Set Pass is used to set up the password for the current user. If you select Logout, you will be logged out of the system. When you are logged out you can see all the available file server in the resource box. You can select any of the file server and then login into that file server.

6. The next button (the one that shows a note) is used to **Send Messages** to other users. This button can be activated by clicking with the mouse or by pressing **<Alt><M>**. This option shows three boxes: Message, Connections, and Resources. Message box is used to type any message to broadcast. Resources show all the users that are currently logged into the system. At the bottom you can see four buttons: NetWare Info, Show Groups, Show Users, and Send. If you select Show Groups button you can see all the available groups in the Resource box. If you receive any message from a user, press the OK button to clear the message.

7. The next button (the one that shows a key) shows **NetWare Settings**. This button can be activated by clicking with the mouse or by pressing **<Alt><S>**. You can turn off message reception from this box. You can also enable or disable the hotkey (default is <F6>) from this box. If the hotkey feature is enabled, User Tools can be activated by just pressing the hotkey.

8. The next two buttons (the one that show 1 and 2) are **User Defined** buttons. These buttons can be activated by clicking with the mouse or by pressing **<Alt><1>** or

<Alt><2>. When you select any of these buttons you can see a command line box. You can define any command in this command line box to activate any application from within the User Tools.

9. The next button (the one with the interrogation sign) is the **Help** button. This button can be activated by clicking with the mouse or by pressing <Alt><H>. You can also get Help menu by pressing **F1**. To close the Help window select "Exit" under the "File" menu option.

Using ElectroText

(You need MS Windows to use Novell ElectroText.)

1. Activate **ElectroText** by clicking on the icon.

2. Select a library that contains the bookshelf of you choice. For example, select **NetWare 3.12 Manuals.**

3. The bookshelf shows the icons for all the books available on the bookshelf. Select *Utilities Reference* manual.

4. Find **FILER** using the outline. Outline is a sort of index for the book. When you view any book in the ElectroText, you will see two windows. One window shows the outline of the book, and the other window shows explanation. If you select any topic in the outline with the cursor, the other window moves to the corresponding page automatically. You can set how the outline appears on the screen from the **Preferences** option from the **File** menu. The outline can appear on left, right, top or bottom of explanation.

5. Find out what kind of administrative tasks can be performed by using the FILER utility.

6. Search for *NetWare*. You can type the word you want to search in the "Search for" box at the bottom of the screen. If you want to search for the word in any particular manual or manuals, hold down the shift key and click the book(s) on the screen. This action will add or remove the box around the book name. If now you execute the search command, ElectroText will only look for the search items

in the books with the box around them. Press the **Execute** button at the bottom to start the search. When the search is over you will see a number next to the book you have selected. This shows the number of times the search item appears in that manual. If you now browse through the manual you will see that the search item is highlighted throughout the manual. Record how many times *NetWare* appears in the *Utilities Reference* manual. Press the **Clear** button to enter a new search item.

7. Use the **HELP** feature of ElectroText. Search for a topic of your interest.

8. Go back to the window that shows all the manuals.

9. Search for *NetWare* through all the manuals. You can select all the manuals by checking the **Select All** option from the **Search** menu. After the search is over you will see a number next to all the books in which the search item was found. This number shows the number of times the search item appears in each book. If you browse through any of these books, you will see that the search item has been highlighted throughout all the manuals. Record how many times this word appears in all manuals.

10. Browse through some other features to get familiar with the different available options in ElectroText. Exit ElectroText after you are finished.

File Server Utilities

File server utilities are executed from the file server console. We have two types of file server utilities:

Console Commands

These are commands you execute from the console prompt. For example: CLS, DOWN, SPOOL. See Appendix A for a list of console commands.

NetWare Loadable Modules (NLMs)

NLMs are programs which work with the NetWare 3.1x operating system to provide additional services. NLMs can be loaded and unloaded from the file server memory without downing the server. They link disk drivers, LAN drivers, name space, and other file server management and enhancement utilities to the operating system.

NetWare 3.12 has four types of loadable modules

- **Disk Drivers** control communication between the operating system and the hard disks. These modules have a .DSK extension. For example ISADISK.DSK.

- **LAN Drivers** control communication between the operating system and the network boards. These modules have a LAN extension. For example TRXNET.LAN.

- **NLM Utilities** allow you to monitor and change configuration options. These modules have a .NLM extension. For example, MONITOR.NLM, INSTALL.NLM, and VREPAIR.NLM

- **Name Space Modules** allow non-DOS file systems to be stored in NetWare volumes. These modules have a .NAM extension. For example, OS2.NAM, and MAC.NAM

Important Management NLM Utilities

INSTALL

The INSTALL utility is used to complete the NetWare 3.12 installation and for maintenance purposes. The following can be done using INSTALL:

- Create the NetWare partition.
- Mirror/duplex hard disks.
- Create volumes.
- Create or edit the file server boot files (AUTOEXEC.NCF and STARTUP.NCF).
- Copy the SYSTEM and PUBLIC files.
- Install and configure products on the server.

MONITOR

MONITOR.NLM is the major utility used to view memory usage and status information. We use the MONITOR utility to view the utilization and overall activity of the file server, cache memory status, connections and their status, disk drives, mounted volumes, LAN drivers, loaded modules, file lock status, and memory usage.

Source Routing Support

Source Routing Support is provided to support IBM hardware and applications. ROUTE.NLM allows NetWare to communicate across IBM Token Ring network bridges. Non-routeable protocols like NetBIOS cannot be routed, they need to use bridges. In an IBM network with source routing bridges, the frame header contains source routing information. ROUTE.NLM enables NetWare to keep track of the source routing information in the frame. To set up a NetWare workstation for source routing, do the following :

1. Load the NetWare TOKEN.LAN driver.
2. Load ROUTE.NLM on the file server.
3. Run ROUTE.COM from the workstation.

Remote Booting

NetWare supports the remote booting of workstations. The user boots the workstation (usually a diskless workstation) from files (boot image files) on the server rather than from a boot disk at the workstation.

You will need to load RPL.NLM (the Remote Program Load NLM) and bind it to the network board if using diskless workstations with the RPL BIOS module (e.g., workstations with Token Ring boards).

For more information, refer to the Novell *Workstation for DOS and Windows* manual.

Review Questions

Q.1. ElectroText is a(n) _____ .

    a. electronic version of NetWare manuals
    b. electronic version of NetWare operating system
    c. NetWare workstation utility
    d. NetWare file server utility

Q.2. NLMs are _____ .

    a. programs that work with NetWare 3.1x operating system to provide additional services
    b. disk drivers
    c. management utilities
    d. programs that provide printing services

Q.3. Which one of the following is not an NLM?

    a. ISADISK.DSK   b. NE2000.LAN
    c. INSTALL.EXE   d. MAC.NAM

Q.4. Remote booting with boot PROM means _____ .

    a. booting the workstation from the file server
    b. booting file server from workstation
    c. booting workstation from boot PROM
    d. booting file server from boot PROM

Q.5. To rename a user, which of the following keys would you use when using SYSCON?

    a. F5 Toggle   b. F1 Help
    c. F3 – modifier   d. DELETE and then INSERT key

Chapter 4   Directory and File Management

NetWare Directory Structure

The NetWare directory structure starts with volume, which is equivalent to the root in the DOS directory structure. All directories and files are created in volume. The server name, volume, directory, subdirectory, and file name constitute a full directory path for a NetWare file and looks like this:

FS1\SYS:APPS\WINDOWS\EXEL\EXCEL.EXE
File server name\Volume:Directory\Subdirectory\Subdirectory\File

We can use either DOS or NetWare commands to move within the directory structure.

NetWare Volumes

As mentioned before, a volume is the highest level in the NetWare directory structure (like the DOS root directory). A volume in the NetWare can be created on the file server's hard disk or on another storage device, such as a CD ROM. A NetWare 3.12 server can support up to 32 TB of hard disk space and up to 64 volumes. Each volume can have up to 32 TB of hard disk space and can span up to 32 disks. The total space in all volumes cannot exceed 32 TB. The first volume on a server must be named SYS. Other volumes can be created using the following rules:

© 1993 - 95 · PC Age, Inc. All Rights Reserved · 20 Audrey Place · Fairfield, NJ 07004 · U.S.A. · Tel: 201-882-5370

- The name must be 2 to 15 characters long.

- The volume name must be followed by a colon (:) when used in path, e.g., SYS:.

- Spaces, commas, back slashes, and periods are not permitted within the volume name.

- Use only the letters A-Z, the numbers zero through nine, and the following symbols: (~), (!), (#), ($), (%), (^), (&), (()), (-), (_), and ({}).

- Two volumes on the same NetWare server cannot have the same name.

- The back slash (\) or the forward slash (/) must be used to separate the NetWare server name from the physical volume name when used in the path.

Chapter 4: Directory and File Management

NetWare-Created Directories

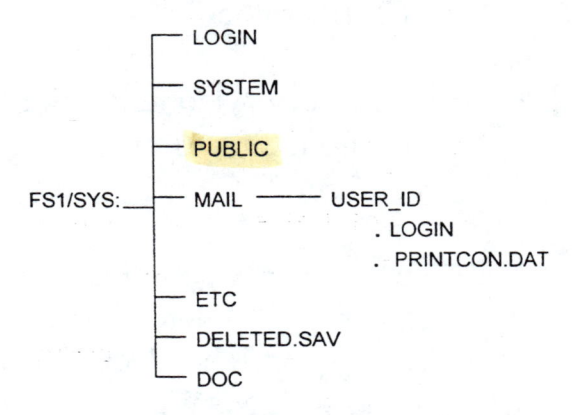

```
                          ┌── LOGIN
                          ├── SYSTEM
                          ├── PUBLIC
              FS1/SYS: ───┼── MAIL ────── USER_ID
                          │                    . LOGIN
                          │                    . PRINTCON.DAT
                          ├── ETC
                          ├── DELETED.SAV
                          └── DOC
```

Figure 4-1 NetWare created directories.

NetWare creates several directories and files during installation. These are:

SYSTEM	Contains the NetWare operating system, the bindery and system files. These utilities are used by the supervisor for administrative tasks.
PUBLIC	Used for general access. It contains utilities that all users can use.
LOGIN	Contains the utilities necessary for logging in.
MAIL	This directory has a subdirectory for each user. NetWare creates a subdirectory for each user using the user's ID number. Each user's subdirectory contains that user's login script and print job configuration.

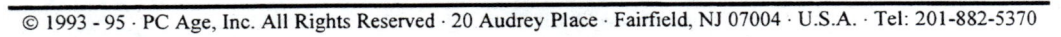

© 1993 - 95 · PC Age, Inc. All Rights Reserved · 20 Audrey Place · Fairfield, NJ 07004 · U.S.A. · Tel: 201-882-5370

4-3

ETC	This directory has the sample files that help in configuring the file server for TCP/IP protocol.
DELETED.SAV	This directory contains all of the deleted files from directories that have been removed.
DOC	This directory contains the electronic version of the NetWare manuals, ElectroText. The electronic version comes with NetWare 3.12 on CD-ROM.

Chapter 4: Directory and File Management

Directories You Should Create on the Server

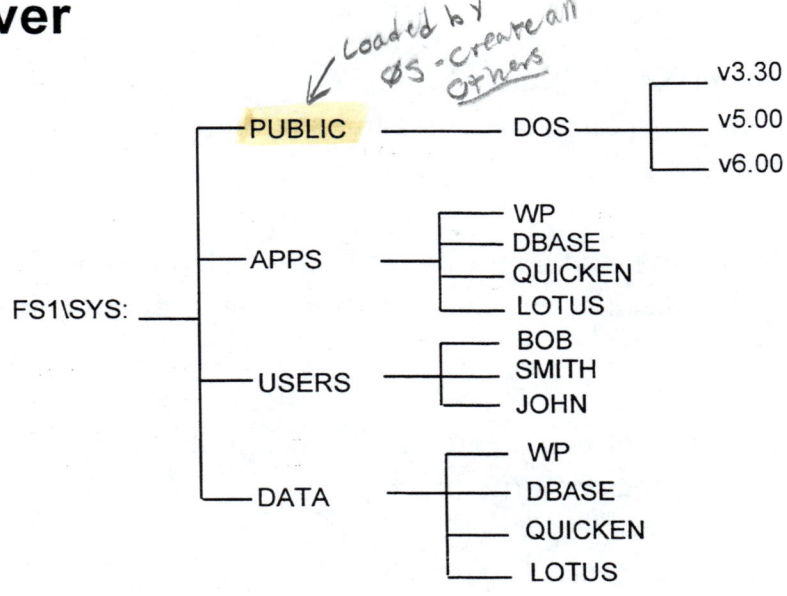

```
                                                    ┌─ v3.30
                  ┌─ PUBLIC ──────── DOS ───────────┤── v5.00
                  │   (Loaded by                    └─ v6.00
                  │    OS - create all
                  │    others)
                  │              ┌─ WP
                  │              ├─ DBASE
                  ├─ APPS ───────┤── QUICKEN
   FS1\SYS: ──────┤              └─ LOTUS
                  │              ┌─ BOB
                  ├─ USERS ──────┤── SMITH
                  │              └─ JOHN
                  │              ┌─ WP
                  │              ├─ DBASE
                  └─ DATA ───────┤── QUICKEN
                                 └─ LOTUS
```

Figure 4-2 Directories user create on the server.

The primary function of a directory is to hold a set of files that belong together. The directory structure should be kept as simple and as logical as possible. There should not be too many levels in the directory structure. Avoid storing any files at the volume (root) level in NetWare. The following rules apply for directories:

- The name must be 2 to 8 characters long. An extension of 1 to 3 characters is allowed. *Just like DOS*

- Spaces, commas, back slashes, and periods are not permitted. *Just like DOS*

- Use only the letters A-Z, the numbers 0 through 9, and the following symbols: (~), (!), (#), ($), (%), (^), (&) (()), (-), (_), and ({}).

© 1993 - 95 · PC Age, Inc. All Rights Reserved · 20 Audrey Place · Fairfield, NJ 07004 · U.S.A. · Tel: 201-882-5370

4-5

- Two subdirectories of the same directory cannot have the same name.

- In NetWare utilities, the back slash (\) is used to separate parts of a path name and can be interchanged with a forward slash (/).

- The volume name is always followed by a colon (:) with an optional separator (\ or /) between it and the first directory name.

It is suggested that you create the following directories to help organize the directory structure.

- Home Directories "USERS" - For users personal files
- Applications - Install All APPS HERE
- DOS Directories - Store different versions of DOS
- Shared Data Area - For Shared data files on the system

Home Directories

Home Directories are for users' personal files. All users home directories should be created under a directory called USERS. You can create a user's home directory when creating the user. Each user is given all rights to his directory, and the user home directory is often named after the user login name, for instance, if a user's login name is SMITH, the user home directory name looks like this:

SYS:USERS\SMITH

Application Directory

For management reasons, it is best to create a directory for applications and install all applications in this directory. The subdirectories for applications contain pure applications files. No user-created files should be stored under this directory. Keeping these files in a logical place makes it easier for the Supervisor to manage upgrades and changes.

DOS Directories

If your users are using different versions of DOS, you should create a directory for each DOS version. If the user boots his workstation with DOS v5.0, for example, he must be executing the external DOS commands from the directory of the same version, otherwise he will get error messages. DOS directories are created under the SYS:PUBLIC directory. The SYS:PUBLIC directory has files (NetWare utilities) available to all network users. By default, all users have appropriate rights to execute commands from the SYS:PUBLIC directory and its subdirectories.

If creating subdirectories for different versions of DOS, use the subdirectory names as shown in figure 4-2. For example, for DOS version 5, the subdirectory name should be v5.00. Then you will be able to use the identifier variable OS_VERSION in the SYSTEM login script to set up the proper search mapping. We will discuss login scripts in later chapters.

Shared Data Area

We can create a data directory to store data files that are shared on the system. Within a data directory, we can then organize the data files in subdirectories that are specific for certain groups.

System Administration NetWare 3.12

Multiple Volume Server

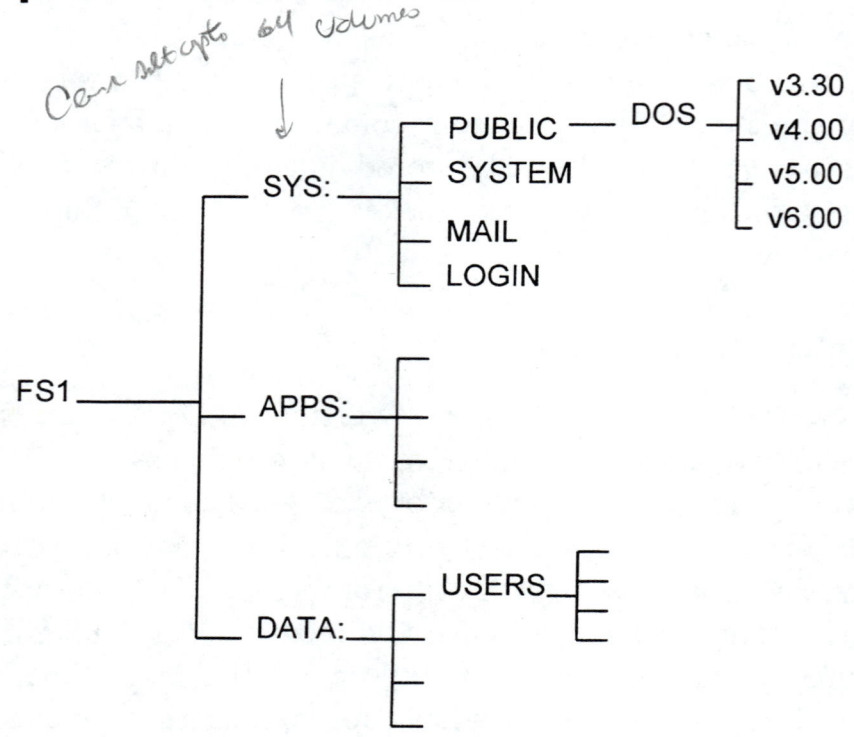

Can set up to 64 volumes

```
FS1 ─┬─ SYS: ─┬─ PUBLIC ─── DOS ─┬─ v3.30
     │        ├─ SYSTEM          ├─ v4.00
     │        ├─ MAIL            ├─ v5.00
     │        └─ LOGIN           └─ v6.00
     │
     ├─ APPS:
     │
     └─ DATA: ─┬─ USERS
              
```

Figure 4-3 Suggested Multiple Directory Structure

Figure 4-3 shows a multiple volume directory structure. Multiple volumes are recommended on a server. Here are some advantages and disadvantages of having multiple volumes versus a single [SYS:] volume.

Advantages

1. If you have multiple volumes, you will not lose everything if one volume fails or gets errors.

2. Making backups is easier because you can make backups of the data volume on a daily basis for instance and backups of APPS once a week (or once a month, as needed).

3. Restoring is also easier if you just need to restore a small volume as compared to a big volume.

4. Rights management is also easier because you can work at the volume level rather than the directory level. For example, you can restrict APPS volume to R F.

Disadvantages

1. In a multiple volume server you may have enough total space available in all volumes but not in the volume where you need it.

2. More drive mappings are necessary. Each volume will require at least one mapping.

3. Multiple volumes are a little more difficult to manage than just one.

Generally it is better to have multiple volumes versus having one big volume [SYS:]. My suggestion is to create a SYS volume of about 64 MB. Do not make the SYS volume too small because your users may not be able to print big jobs. You may also need more space in the SYS volume when installing optional products from Novell or additional DOS versions. Create the APPS volume according to your needs. Create the DATA volume according to your needs. A good strategy is to leave some free space in the NetWare partition (do not add all of the available partition space to the volumes). This free space can be added to any volume when needed.

For example, if you have 1 GB NetWare partition, create the volumes as follows:

SYS volume	64 MB
APPS volume	250 MB
DATA volume	400 MB

After you create all the volumes, you still have 286 MB space free in the NetWare partition. This free space can be added to any volume later. Remember you can add space to any volume any time but cannot reduce a volume's size once it is created. To decrease a volume's size you have to delete the volume and recreate it with the smaller size.

Creating Directories on the Server

We can use either DOS commands or NetWare's FILER utility to create directories on the file server.

Using DOS to Create Directories

We can use the following DOS commands to create or manage directories:

MD

RD

CD

Using DOS commands to manage directories and files is simple because we are familiar with them already. However, NetWare commands are much more powerful than DOS commands. For example, the FILER utility allows you to copy, delete, or move an entire directory structure. Doing the same task using DOS commands would require several steps.

Utilities used for Viewing Server Information

The SLIST and FILER utilities are used to view the file server information.

SLIST

The SLIST utility can be used to view the server's name, network address, node address, status and the total number of servers found. This utility can be used to view information about a single file server or a group of file servers. To view information about a single file server type the name of the server after the SLIST command. To view information about a group of file servers wildcard characters can be used.

Using the NetWare FILER Utility to Create Directories

To create a directory using the FILER utility, follow these steps:

1. Log in as a Supervisor.

2. At the command line type
    >FILER

3. An "Available Topics" menu will appear. Choose the "Select Current Directory" option. An empty box displaying the current directory path will appear.

4. You now have two options:

   i. You can type the directory path you want. Press <Enter> after typing the path.
      OR
   ii. You can press <Ins> to list the current directories available. Select the desired directory and subdirectory. Press <Esc> to go to the path NetWare is entering for you as you are selecting. Now you can press <Enter>.

5. Select "Directory Contents" from the "Available Topics" menu. A list of directory's contents will be displayed.

6. To create a subdirectory press <Ins>.

7. As prompted, enter a new subdirectory name and press <Enter>.

Removing a Directory Using the FILER Utility

1. Select "Directory Contents" from the "Available Topics" menu. A list of current subdirectories and files appear.

2. Highlight the name of the directory you want to delete and press <Del>. You will be given several options, including deleting the files in the subdirectory or deleting the entire directory structure.

Chapter 4: Directory and File Management

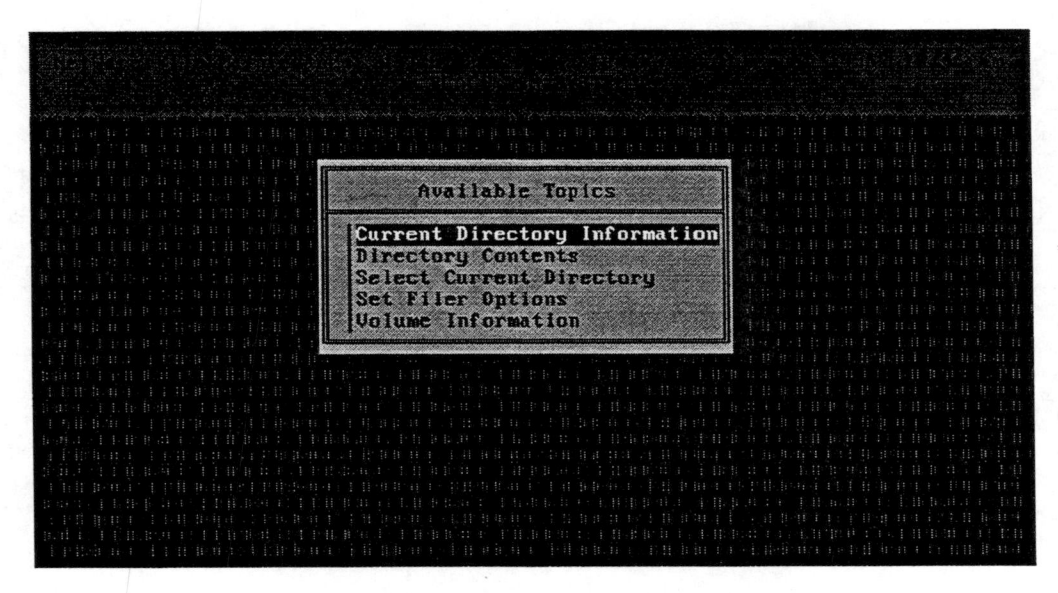

Figure 4-4(a) FILER Utility: Main Manu

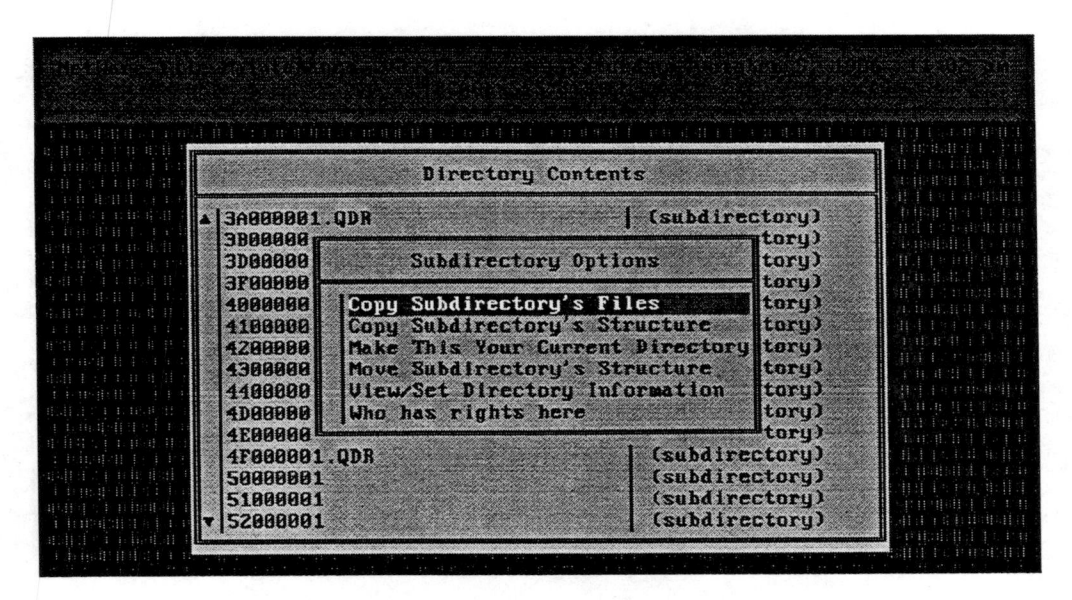

Figure 4-4(b) FILER Utility: Directory Contents - Subdirectory Options

System Administration NetWare 3.12

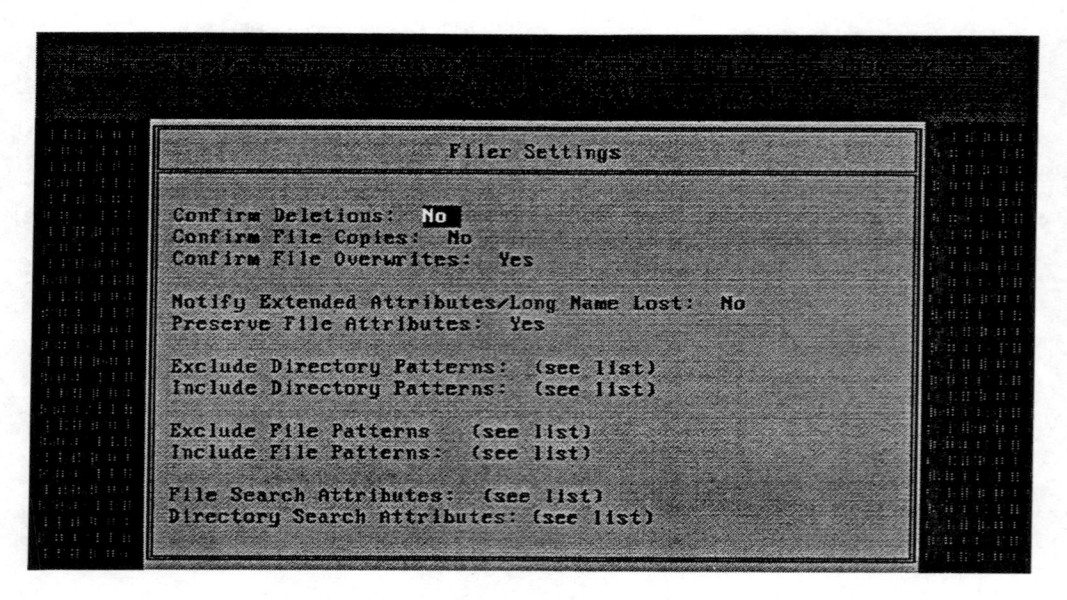

```
                    Filer Settings

   Confirm Deletions: No
   Confirm File Copies: No
   Confirm File Overwrites: Yes

   Notify Extended Attributes/Long Name Lost: No
   Preserve File Attributes: Yes

   Exclude Directory Patterns: (see list)
   Include Directory Patterns: (see list)

   Exclude File Patterns: (see list)
   Include File Patterns: (see list)

   File Search Attributes: (see list)
   Directory Search Attributes: (see list)
```

Figure 4-4(c) FILER Utility: Set Filer Option

```
              Available Topics
        Current Direc
        Directory Con         Volume Information
        Select Curren
        Set Filer Opt   Server Name:              PCAGE
        Volume Inform   Volume Name:              SYS
                        Volume Type:              fixed
                        Total KBytes:             435,868
                        Kilobytes Available:      325,636
                        Maximum Directory Entries: 11,872
                        Directory Entries Available: 6,435
```

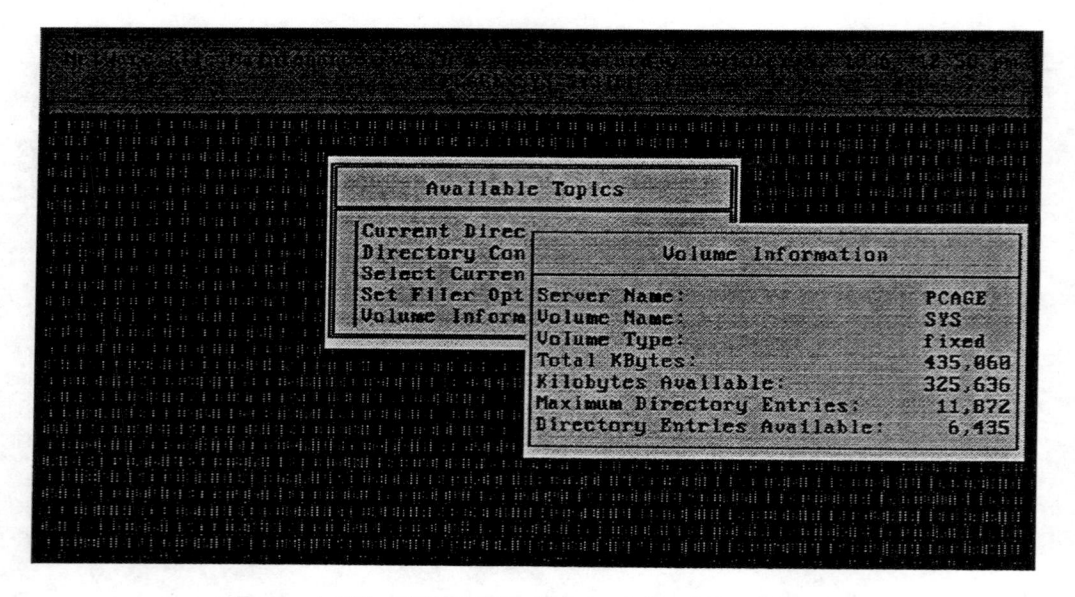

Figure 4-4(d) FILER Utility: Volume Information Screen

Utilities Used for Viewing Volume Information

The VOLINFO, CHKVOL, and FILER utilities can be used to view information about volumes.

VOLINFO

VOLINFO is used to view information about the volumes on the file server. This utility is used to see how storage space is being used, and how many more directories can be created on each volume.

CHKVOL

CHKVOL is used to display the volume space usage information. This information is useful to determine when a volume is approaching full capacity. The command syntax is:

    CHKVOL [*path*] /c

Wildcard characters can be used for displaying information on multiple volumes.

FILER

FILER is used to view information about the current volume such as server name, volume name, volume type, size, space available, and maximum directory entries.

Utilities Used to View or Change Information About Directories

LISTDIR, NDIR, CHKDIR, DSPACE, RENDIR and the FILER utilities are used to view information about directories.

LISTDIR

LISTDIR is used to view the subdirectories of a directory, the **Inherited Right Mask (IRM)** of each subdirectory, the effective rights of each subdirectory, and the creation date of each subdirectory and subsequent subdirectories. The following options are available with the LISTDIR command:

ALL
Rights
Effective rights
Date
Time
Subdirectories

```
F:\> listdir f:\system /all

The sub-directory structure of PCAGE/SYS:SYSTEM
Date      Time    Inherited    Effective   Directory
-------------------------------------------------------------------------
9-13-93   9:10p  [SRWCEMFA]  [SRWCEMFA]  -> TEST1
11-10-93  8:18p  [SRWCEMFA]  [SRWCEMFA]  -> 05000008.QDR
8-11-93   11:45a [SRWCEMFA]  [SRWCEMFA]  -> DR
8-11-93   11:45a [SRWCEMFA]  [SRWCEMFA]  -> TSA
8-11-93   11:45a [SRWCEMFA]  [SRWCEMFA]  -> DIBI
11-06-93  1:31p  [SRWCEMFA]  [SRWCEMFA]  -> 08000007.QDR
11-06-93  1:31p  [SRWCEMFA]  [SRWCEMFA]  -> 09000003.QDR
10-04-93  8:17p  [SRWCEMFA]  [SRWCEMFA]  -> MATT
11-06-93  1:45p  [SRWCEMFA]  [SRWCEMFA]  -> 0C000003
9-19-93   9:16p  [SRWCEMFA]  [SRWCEMFA]  -> SYS
10-16-93  1:47p  [SRWCEMFA]  [SRWCEMFA]  ->    APPS
10-16-93  1:48p  [SRWCEMFA]  [SRWCEMFA]  ->    NORTON
10-16-93  1:53p  [SRWCEMFA]  [SRWCEMFA]  ->    QUICKEN
11-11-93  6:38p  [SRWCEMFA]  [SRWCEMFA]  -> 0B000006
8-14-93   4:16p  [SRWCEMFA]  [SRWCEMFA]  -> BACKUP
10-09-93  1:14p  [SRWCEMFA]  [SRWCEMFA]  -> TEMP5
16 sub-directories found

F:\>
```

Figure 4-5 The NetWare LISTDIR Utility with /All Switch.

NDIR

Use NDIR to view information about files, subdirectories, and directories on network drives.

NDIR can also be used to view files and subdirectories created by Macintosh machines (marked with a lower case "m"), OS/2 machines (marked with lower case "o"), or an NFS machines (marked with lower case "n"). For example NDIR/MAC is entered to view Macintosh files in the current directory.

Files

NDIR is used to view file information including names, size in bytes, dates and times files were last modified, dates files were last accessed, files that have the archive bit set, dates files were created or copied, and file owners. Use the NDIR/FO command to view information for files only.

Subdirectories

NDIR with /SUB option is used to view subdirectory information such as names, date created, Inherited Rights Mask, effective rights, and owner or creator. The command line option SUBdirectory is used to view subdirectories and subsequent subdirectories.

Directories

Use the command line option DO to display directories only.

Chapter 4: Directory and File Management

f:> NDIR/?

usage:	NDIR [path] [/option...]
path:	[path] [filename] [,filename, ...] (up to 16 in chain)
options:	[format], [flag], [sortspec], [restriction], [FO] (files only), [DO] (directories only), [SUBdirectories], [Continuous], [HELP]
format:	DATES, RIGHTS, MACintosh, LONGnames
flag:	[NOT] RO, S, A, X, H, SY, T, I, P, RA, WA, CI, DI, RI
sortspec:	[REVerse] SORT [OWner], [SIze], [UPdate], [CReate], [ACcess], [ARchive], [UNsorted]
restriction:	OWner <operator> <name>
	SIze <operator> <number>
	UPdate <operator> <date>
	CReate <operator> <date>
	ACcess <operator> <date>
	ARchive <operator> <date>
	operator: [NOT] LEss than, GReater than, EQual to, BEFore, AFTer

To search filenames equivalent to any of the capitalized KEYWORD options shown above, the filename must be preceded by a drive letter or path.

Figure 4-6 NDIR Options.

Sample NDIR Screen

FS2/VOL1:APPS\DBWD>ndir /sort update update LE 08-31-90

Files:		Size	Last Updated	Flags	Owner
REMM	SYS	15,645	11-20-87 2:14p	[Rw----------------]	SUPERVISOR
PARTNDX	DBF	4,730	3-01-88 2:50p	[Rw----------------]	SUPERVISOR
S	BAT	18	7-08-88 2:03p	[Rw----------------]	SUPERVISOR
OSLAB	LBL	1,034	8-18-88 8:52a	[Rw----------------]	SUPERVISOR
OSLABDS	LBL	1,034	8-18-88 9:01a	[Rw----------------]	SUPERVISOR
TAPRCT	DBT	513	11-10-88 4:43p	[Rw----------------]	SUPERVISOR
TAPPART	DBF	1,213	11-11-88 1:03p	[Rw----------------]	SUPERVISOR
TAPODR	DBF	6,492	11-21-88 2:57p	[Rw----------------]	SUPERVISOR
TAPRCT	DBF	6,045	12-12-88 10:22a	[Rw----------------]	SUPERVISOR
MENU2	MNU	293	1-16-89 9:28a	[Rw----------------]	SUPERVISOR
MENU1	MNU	277	1-16-89 10:01a	[Rw----------------]	SUPERVISOR
SNIPESYN	DAT	50	1-16-89 10:12a	[Rw----------------]	SUPERVISOR
SNIPEINI	DAT	55	1-16-89 10:12a	[Rw----------------]	SUPERVISOR
OPLAB2	DBF	503	1-18-89 2:29p	[Rw----------------]	SUPERVISOR
FD	DBF	1,923	1-25-89 2:44p	[Rw----------------]	SUPERVISOR
TAPPART	NTX	2,048	1-25-89 3:37p	[Rw----------------]	SUPERVISOR
TAPPTWT	NTX	2,048	1-25-89 3:37p	[Rw----------------]	SUPERVISOR
TAPOTWT	NTX	2,048	1-25-89 3:37p	[Rw----------------]	SUPERVISOR
TAPRTWT	NTX	2,048	1-25-89 3:37p	[Rw----------------]	SUPERVISOR
MENU_Z	BAT	12	1-26-89 11:28a	[Rw----------------]	SUPERVISOR
E	BAT	106	1-26-89 12:04p	[Rw----------------]	SUPERVISOR
CUSMEM	MEM	4,176	2-13-89 12:29p	[Rw----------------]	SUPERVISOR
ODRPART	NTX	12,288	4-21-89 7:29a	[Rw----------------]	SUPERVISOR
JOHN	BAT	15	5-08-89 11:07a	[Rw----------------]	SUPERVISOR
VENDOR	DBT	514	5-17-89 2:50p	[Rw----------------]	SUPERVISOR
TLAB	DBF	8,495	7-12-89 2:50p	[Rw----------------]	SUPERVISOR
PHONE	DBF	8,080	7-14-89 1:41p	[Rw----------------]	SUPERVISOR
LYN	BAT	14	8-15-89 8:58a	[Rw----------------]	SUPERVISOR
LEON	BAT	15	8-15-89 2:50p	[Rw----------------]	SUPERVISOR
WPQUE	SYS	2,550	9-01-89 9:45a	[Rw----------------]	SUPERVISOR
CALLMM	BAT	41	9-01-89 9:59a	[Rw----------------]	SUPERVISOR
NCMAIN	EXE	139,274	10-23-89 3:00p	[Rw-A------------]	SUPERVISOR
NC	EXE	3,100	10-23-89 3:00p	[Rw-A------------]	SUPERVISOR
TELELAB	EXE	177,402	11-06-89 3:41p	[Rw-A------------]	SUPERVISOR
XC	BAT	390	11-07-89 7:40a	[Rw----------------]	SUPERVISOR
POINFVEN	NTX	8,192	4-17-90 8:48a	[Rw----------------]	SUPERVISOR
CUSTOMER	DBT	4,608	4-18-90 4:33p	[Rw----------------]	SUPERVISOR
NSQTYFAC	DBF	235	5-21-90 10:53a	[Rw----------------]	SUPERVISOR
TRANSSEF	DBF	217	6-25-90 8:27a	[Rw----------------]	SUPERVISOR
OACTPART	NTX	24,576	7-03-90 7:52a	[Rw----------------]	SUPERVISOR
OPARTACT	NTX	24,576	7-03-90 9:15a	[Rw----------------]	SUPERVISOR
POSTREP	DBF	1,401	8-06-90 10:30a	[Rw----------------]	SUPERVISOR
POINFCO2	NTX	6,144	8-27-90 12:04p	[Rw----------------]	SUPERVISOR

1,096,216 bytes in 43 files
1,269,760 bytes in 310 blocks

Figure 4-7 Sample NDIR screen.

CHKDIR

Use CHKDIR to get directory space limitation information for the file server, volume, and directory, the maximum storage capacity of the file server in kilobytes, the number of kilobytes currently in use, the number of kilobytes available on the volume and in the specified directory.

```
F:\SYSTEM>chkdir

Directory Space Limitation Information For:
PCAGE\SYS:SYSTEM

    Maximum      In Use       Available
    111,308 K    51,348 K     59,960 K       Volume Size
                 4,340 K      59,960 K       \SYSTEM
```

Figure 4-8 The NetWare CHKDIR Utility.

DSPACE

Use DSPACE to limit the disk space on volumes or in directories. SYSCON and USERDEF can also be used to limit disk space on volumes but they do not limit disk space in directories.

```
Novell Disk Usage Utility   v3.56      Friday  October 8, 1993   7:54 pm
                   User SUPERVISOR On File Server PCAGE
```

```
            Available Options
        Change File Server
      ⇒ User Restrictions
        Directory Restrictions
```

Figure 4-9 (a) The NetWare DSPACE Utility.

System Administration NetWare 3.12

```
┌─────────────────────────────────────────────┐
│      User Disk Space Limitation Information │
│                                             │
│   User:        BOB                          │
│   Volume       SYS                          │
│   Limit Space:              No              │
│   Available:                Kbytes          │
│   In Use:                 0 Kbytes          │
└─────────────────────────────────────────────┘
```

```
┌─────────────────────────────────────────────┐
│   Directory Disk Space Limitation Information │
│                                             │
│   Path Space Limit:              Kilobytes  │
│   Limit Space:  No                          │
│   Directory Space Limit:         Kilobytes  │
│   Currently Available:     59957 Kilobytes  │
└─────────────────────────────────────────────┘
```

Figure 4-9 (b) The NetWare DSPACE Utility.

RENDIR

(handwritten note: Not Automatically Updated.)

RENDIR is used to change the name of a directory. When we rename a directory, the users retain their rights. The login scripts must be changed to reflect the new name. The user must have the modify right in the directory to rename a subdirectory in that directory. The command syntax for using RENDIR is

   RENDIR [path\] dirname [TO] new name

Examples:

1. To rename a subdirectory

    RENDIR DOS5 DOS6

   The above command changes the directory name DOS5 to DOS6.

© 1993 - 95 · PC Age, Inc. All Rights Reserved · 20 Audrey Place · Fairfield, NJ 07004 · U.S.A. · Tel: 201-882-5370

Chapter 4: Directory and File Management

2. To rename a directory on another volume

   RENDIR G:\DATABASE TO DBWD

   The above command changes the directory DATABASE on another volume to DBWD.

3. To rename a directory on another volume using the volume name.

   RENDIR PCAGE1\SYS:DOC\NOTES TO NOTES.OLD

System Administration NetWare 3.12

Managing Files with the FILER Utility

The FILER utility manages volume, directory, and file information. Some additional tasks that can be done with the FILER utility include marking multiple files to copy, deleting and moving files and directories, deleting entire directory structures, and setting up filters.

Copying Directories and Files using the NCOPY Command

The NCOPY command is used to copy file and directories. The DOS COPY command and XCOPY command will also work. NCOPY is preferred over these DOS commands in the network environment because:

- It can copy NetWare's extended file information.

- It can notify the user if extended attributes or name space information cannot be copied.

- It can verify that the copy was accurate.

- It has the ability to copy files using NetWare volume names.

Managing Deleted Files with SALVAGE and PURGE

SALVAGE

The **SALVAGE** utility is used to recover deleted files, view all deleted files, and to purge files. Every deleted file is kept in the same directory it was in just before it was deleted. If the directory is deleted, the directory and files are stored in a hidden directory named DELETED.SAV located in the root directory of the volume.

```
NetWare File Salvage Utility v3.56      Friday October 8, 1993  7:54 pm
              SUPERVISOR On PCAGE/SYS:DELETED.SAV
```

Main Menu Options
Salvage From Deleted Directories
Select Current Directory
Set Salvage Options
View/Recover Deleted Files

Figure 4-10 The NetWare SALVAGE Utility.

PURGE

PURGE is used to permanently delete previously erased files. When the file server needs space for new files, it automatically purges recoverable files beginning with the oldest deleted file. The user can control which files are deleted first by using PURGE and SALVAGE regularly.

Review Questions

Q.1. The highest level of directory structure in NetWare is called a _____.

    a. Volume   b. NetWare Partition

    c. SYS Volume   d. root directory

Q.2. Which one of the following directories is not created by NetWare during the installation?

    a. LOGIN   b. SYSTEM

    c. USERS   d. PUBLIC

Q.3. Which one of the following is not created during the NetWare installation process?

    a. PUBLIC   b. MAIL

    c. ETC   d. APPS

Q.4. Which of the following directories is suggested by Novell?

    a. PUBLIC   b. USERS

    c. MAIL   d. SYSTEM

Chapter 4: Directory and File Management

Q.5. You should have more than one volumes because _____ .

    a. you will have more disk space
    b. you will not loose every thing in case of volume failure
    c. this is a Novell requirement
    d. SYS volume cannot be larger than 1 GB

Q.6. The main NetWare utility for file and directory management is _____ .

    a. FILER   b. SYS
    c. NDIR   d. DSPACE

Q.7. NDIR cannot be used to view _____ .

    a. DOS directories   b. NetWare directories
    c. NetWare files   d. Macintosh files

Q.8. What commands would you use to delete files in a network? (select all that are true)

    a. DEL   b. NDEL
    c. ERASE   d. PURGE

Hands-On Exercises

Understanding Logging In

Use the following commands to connect your workstation to the file server and to login:

SLIST, LOGIN, USERLIST, SEND, CASTOFF, CASTON, LOGOUT, WHOAMI and SESSION.

- Use the USERLIST command with the switch that shows you node addresses of the current users.

- Use the SESSION utility to view current users and send them messages.

Understanding the Directory Structure

- Use DOS directory commands like DIR, and CD to get familiar with the NetWare directory structure.

- Create a directory under SYS:\USERS. Use your login name as the directory name. Use the DOS MD command to create the directory.

- Use the following NetWare commands:
  CHKDIR, CHKVOL, LISTDIR, NDIR, RENDIR, VOLINFO.

Using the DSPACE Utility

- Go to your home directory.
- Use DSPACE to limit your home directory's disk space to 2MB.

Using the SALVAGE Utility

- Create a file in your home directory. Type:
  >copy con temp.txt
  This is my file
  ^Z

View the directory using NDIR. The file temp.txt should be there. Now delete this file and then use the SALVAGE utility to recover it.

# Chapter 5	Drive Mappings

Drive Mappings

Drive mapping is simply assigning a letter of the alphabet to a NetWare volume or directory. By assigning or mapping a letter of the alphabet to a NetWare volume or directory, you can easily access it without typing the complete path. It also allows DOS or DOS applications to use a NetWare volume or directory as a local drive.

NetWare recognizes three types of drives: **Local**, **Network**, and **Search**.

Network Drives

Like DOS, NetWare also uses letters of the alphabet as drive pointers. These letters identify logical locations within the system's directory structure (not just physical locations as is the case for DOS).

Drive letters not used by local devices can be used by network drives. NetWare 3.12 requires the LASTDRIVE=Z command in the CONFIG.SYS file (if using NetWare DOS Requester (VLM.EXE)). If the workstation has three local drives A, B, and C, the letters D through Z will be available for mapping as a network drives.

With earlier versions of NetWare (2.x to 3.11) Novell provided NETx as a NetWare shell. If you are using NETx instead of VLM.EXE, your CONFIG.SYS must not have the LASTDRIVE=Z command. If you are not using the LASTDRIVE command and using NETx, some versions of DOS by default use drives A through E as local drives. In this situation, letters F through Z are available as network drives.

Note: Workstation installation program puts **FIRST NETWORK DRIVE=F** command in NET.CFG file and **LASTDRIVE=Z** command in CONFIG.SYS. That is the reason your first network drive is F. The letter F (or first network drive letter) is automatically assigned (mapped) to the LOGIN directory on the SYS volume of the server you first connect or log in.

Chapter 5: Drive Mappings

Local Drives	Network Drives
A : 1	D : 4
B : 2	E : 5
C : 3	F : 6
	G : 7
	H : 8
	I : 9
	J : 10
	16 K : 11
	15 L : 12
	14 M : 13
	13 N : 14
A total of 16	12 O : 15
network drives	11 P : 16
(starting with Z)	10 Q : 17
are available as	9 R : 18
search drives	8 S : 19
	7 T : 20
	6 U : 21
	5 V : 22
	4 W : 23
	3 X : 24
	2 Y : 25
	1 Z : 26

Figure 5-1 Local, Network and Search Drives

The MAP command is used to view or assign network drive pointers to directories.

    F:\>MAP

shows current drive mappings for the workstation.

Network Drive Mapping

MAP drive:= directory path
maps the specified drive (letter) to the given directory.

Example:

    MAP H:= SYS:USERS/JOHN

MAP ROOT drive:= directory path
creates a pseudo root at the specified path.

    MAP NEXT path

maps the next available drive to a specified path.

You can use the DOS CD command on network drives, but it will change the current drive mapping.

Example:

    G:\APPS\WP>CD..
    G:\APPS>

G: was mapped to the APPS\WP subdirectory, but after using the CD command it is mapped to the APPS directory.

Search Drives

The DOS PATH command is used to access executable files that are located in another directory. DOS searches for executable files first in the workstation RAM, then in the current directory, and then in directories specified in the PATH statement.

If the file is not found in any of these above directories a "Bad command or file name" message appears on the screen.

A search drive allows DOS to find executable files on a network directory.

Search drives are created and inserted in the DOS path statement with the MAP command. Each user can have up to 16 search drives (S1 - S16). When the MAP command is used to create a search drive, the NetWare automatically assigns a drive letter starting with Z: (up to K:, for a total of 16) to that search directory. NetWare assigns a drive letter to the search directory because DOS does not recognize a NetWare directory path such as PCAGE\SYS:PUBLIC.

Search Drive Mapping

Like network drive mapping assignments, MAP commands are used for search drive mappings.

Examples:

    MAP INS S1:=PCAGE\SYS:PUBLIC

creates a search drive and inserts it into the first search position.

    MAP S2:=PCAGE\SYS:PUBLIC\MSDOS

creates a search drive and replaces the current search directory at the second search position with the new search drive.

    MAP S16:=PCAGE\SYS:APPS\WP

creates a search drive and places it to the next available search position.

Note: Search drives are added in consecutive order. For example, if you specify S16 in search mapping and only S1-S4 are used, NetWare will convert S16 to S5.

Search Mappings and the DOS PATH Environment

Let's assume that a workstation's current PATH statement is as follows:

    PATH=C:\;C:\DOS;C:\WP

The user on that workstation creates the following search mappings:

    MAP S1:=SYS:PUBLIC

    MAP S2:=SYS:PUBLIC\DOS

    MAP S3:=SYS:APPS\NC

NetWare will assign a letter Z: to SYS:PUBLIC, Y: to SYS:PUBLIC\DOS and X: to SYS:APPS\NC. Each of these search mappings will replace the search directory in the PATH statement, i.e., Z: will replace C:\, Y: will replace C:\DOS, and X:

will replace C:\WP. If the user types PATH command on the workstation, he will see:

    PATH=Z:.;Y:.;X:.

(DOS will not search for executable files in the C:\;C:\DOS; C:\WP directories anymore.)

If this user logs out from the network, his network search mappings will be deleted, and his local PATH statement is also lost.

If the user wants to keep the DOS PATH local environment, he should use the INS option with the MAP command, for example:

    MAP INS S1:=SYS:PUBLIC

    MAP INS S2:=SYS:PUBLIC\DOS

    MAP INS S3:=SYS:APPS\NC

Now his PATH statement will be like this:

    PATH=Z:.;Y:.;X:.;C:\;C:\DOS;C:\WP

If this user logs out, his network search mappings will be deleted but he will still have his local PATH environment.

Note: If you want to search directories specified in PATH command first, use MAP S16 for all NetWare directories instead of MAP INS.

Deleting A Mapping

To delete a MAP definition, use the MAP command as follows:

MAP DEL drive: or MAP REM drive:

Examples:

    MAP DEL G:

    or

    MAP REM G:

Note: All users mappings are lost when user logs out. All MAP commands should be placed in a login script, so they will be executed each time the user logs in. We will discuss login scripts in chapter 9.

Review Questions

Q.1. Drive mapping is _____ .

    a. assigning letters of the alphabet to logical locations of a NetWare directory structure

    b. assigning letters of the alphabet to physical locations of a NetWare directory structure

    c. searching for executable files in other directories

    d. assigning F: to SYS volume

Q.2. You can map letter A to a NetWare directory.

    a. true   b. false

Q.3. Which one of the following mappings is not correct?

    a. MAP A:=SYS:PUBLIC\DOS

    b. MAP F:=FS1/SYS:SYSTEM

    c. MAP G:SYS:=SYSTEM

    d. MAP ROOT H:=SYS:USERS\BOB

Q.4. To protect your DOS PATH environment, you should use the _____ option with your MAP command.

    a. INSERT   b. NEXT
    c. S16   d. Z:

Q.5. Which one of the following is not related to search mapping?

    a. INSERT   b. NEXT
    c. S16   d. Z:

Q.6. If you want to search DOS directories first and then NetWare directories, which of the following options would you use with the MAP command?

    a. S16   b. INSERT
    c. NEXT   d. MAP

Q.7. If you want to search NetWare directories first and then DOS directories, which of the following would you use with the MAP command?

    a. S16   b. INSERT
    c. NEXT   d. MAP

Q.8. If H: is mapped to USERS\BOB and you use DOS **CD ..** command, then H: will be mapped to _____.

    a. USERS\BOB   b. USERS

    c. C:\USERS\BOB   d. \BOB

Hands-On Exercise

Understanding Drive Mappings

- Map drive P: to your home directory (use the map command to check it).

- Delete the drive P: mapping, and re-map to drive H:. (You should not be in drive P: when deleting it. Go to drive F: and then delete the drive P: mapping.)

- Map drive H: to your home directory with the ROOT option. Do you see any difference in the prompt?

- Remove the ROOT mapping.

- Map search drives: S1 to PUBLIC and S2 to PUBLIC\MSDOS.

Chapter 6   Setting Up Users and Groups

Users

Any person allowed to work on the Network is called a **User**. Each user needs an identity or username to work on the network. Once a username exists as an object in the file server bindery, the user can login to the file server with that username and access the network. Associated with users are optional passwords, restrictions, login scripts, and rights. These topics will be discussed in the following chapters.

Groups

Groups provide a way to simplify network administration by dealing with users collectively rather than individually. All users automatically become members of the group EVERYONE. We can also create other groups if two or more users use the same applications, printer, print queues, and have similar needs for information. We can also use groups to simplify trustee assignments, etc. By using groups, we can execute as many commands as possible in the system login scripts. This way we do not have to create a user login script for each user. This simplifies network administration.

Distributed Network Management

User Account Managers and Workgroup Managers can be assigned users and groups to manage. User Account Managers and Workgroup Managers are usually the most skilled users and are used for distributing the Network Management tasks so that the Supervisor can devote more of his or her time to actual troubleshooting.

Workgroup Manager

Although the Workgroup Managers' responsibilities are very similar to the responsibilities of the Supervisor, they do not entirely replace the Supervisor's role.

What Workgroup Managers Can Do

Workgroup Managers can create users and groups and add users to the groups. Workgroup Managers can also delete users they have created.

Workgroup Managers must be assigned directory trustee rights in order to assign or modify directory trustee rights or disk space restrictions.

What Workgroup Managers Can't Do

Workgroup Managers cannot assign rights that they do not have. They cannot assign a user equivalent to Supervisor. They cannot create another Workgroup Manager. They cannot manage users or groups they have not created unless they are the User Account Manager for those users and groups. They cannot modify their own login restrictions unless they have the management rights of their own accounts.

Chapter 6: Setting Up Users and Groups

User Account Manager

User Account Managers have rights to manage certain user accounts and groups. Workgroup Managers automatically become User Account Managers for those users they create.

What User Account Managers Can Do

User Account Managers can delete their managed users and groups, and assign managed users to a managed group or to a user account manager.

User Account Managers can modify account balances, account restrictions, change passwords, modify login scripts, and change security equivalencies and station restrictions.

If the User Account Manager has sufficient file rights in the directory structure, he can also assign directory trustee rights and disk space restrictions.

What User Account Managers Can't Do

A user account manager cannot create users and groups and cannot assign managed users to a group that he does not manage.

Console Operator

The Supervisor creates a Console Operator using the SYSCON utility. A console operator may be a user or a group (all members). A Console Operator has rights to do the following using the FCONSOLE utility:

- Broadcast messages to users

© 1993 - 95 · PC Age, Inc. All Rights Reserved · 20 Audrey Place · Fairfield, NJ 07004 · U.S.A. · Tel: 201-882-5370

- Change the system date and time
- Enable or disable login for additional users
- Enable or disable the Transaction Tracking System
- Access connection information

A Console Operator cannot clear connections and down the file server. These tasks are only for Supervisor or equivalent users.

Chapter 6: Setting Up Users and Groups

Utilities for Creating Users and Groups

The SYSCON Utility

SYSCON is the main utility to create users and groups. We can also create login scripts and assign rights and login restrictions, etc. Most of the time the only utility LAN Administrators use is SYSCON.

The following tasks can be done in SYSCON:

- Installing Accounting
- Creating users and groups
- Assigning trustee rights, passwords, and login restrictions
- Designating Workgroup Managers and Account Managers
- Creating system and user login scripts, etc.

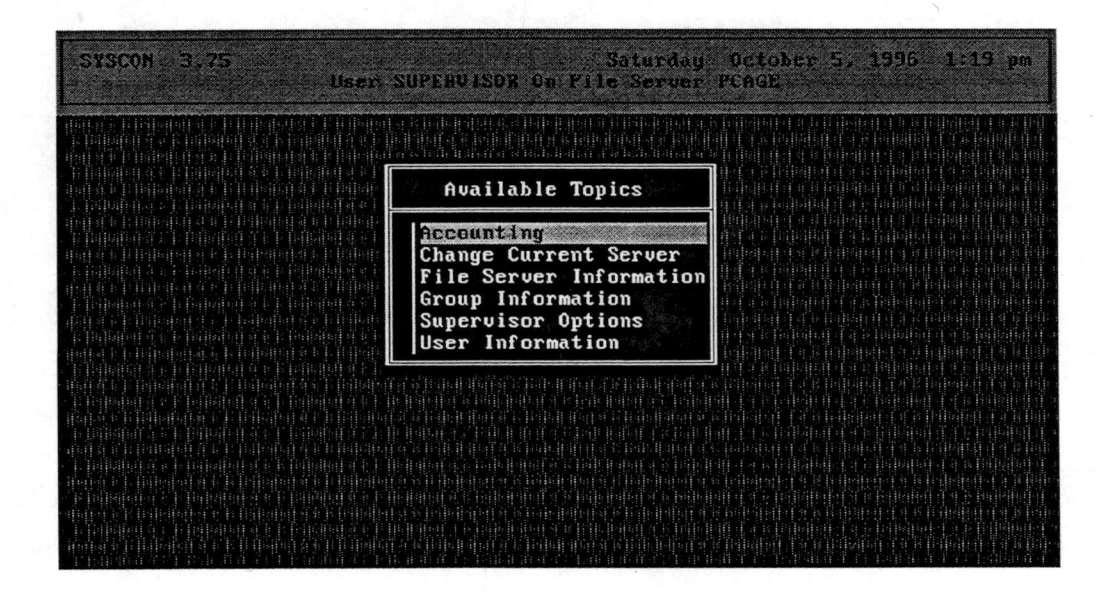

```
SYSCON 3.75                          Saturday October 5, 1996  1:19 pm
             User SUPERVISOR On File Server PCAGE

                         ┌─ Available Topics ─┐
                         │ Accounting         │
                         │ Change Current Server │
                         │ File Server Information │
                         │ Group Information  │
                         │ Supervisor Options │
                         │ User Information   │
                         └────────────────────┘
```

Figure 6-1(a) SYSCON Utility: Main Menu.

© 1993 - 95 · PC Age, Inc. All Rights Reserved · 20 Audrey Place · Fairfield, NJ 07004 · U.S.A. · Tel: 201-882-5370

6-5

System Administration NetWare 3.12

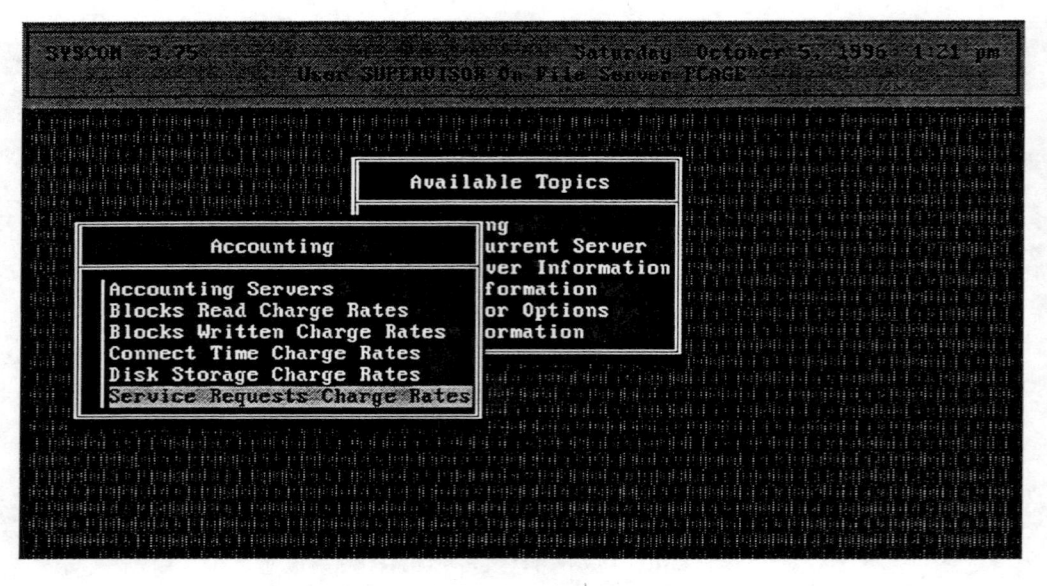

Figure 6-1(b) SYSCON Utility: Accounting Menu

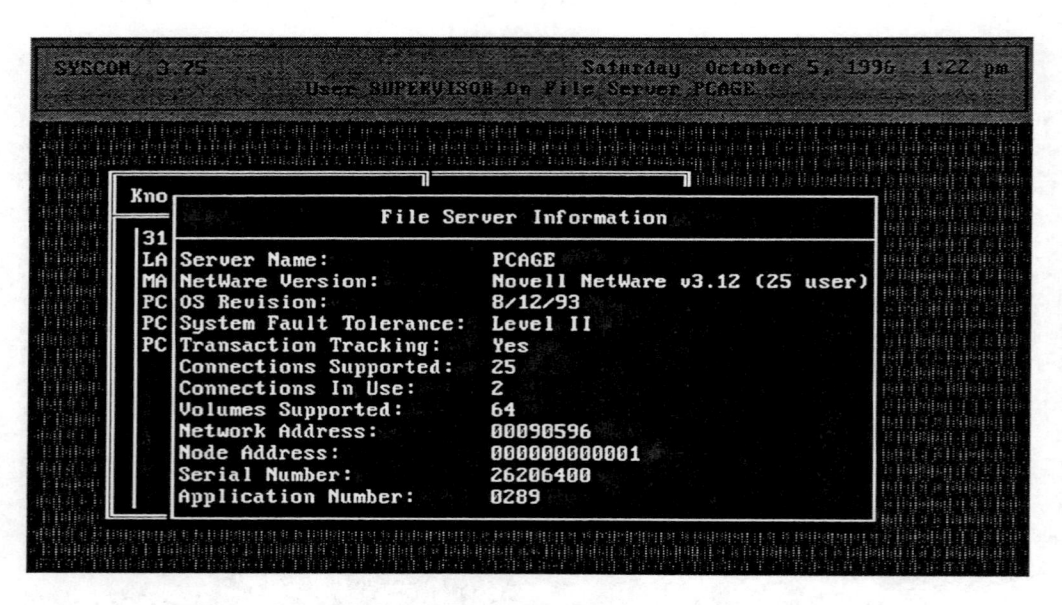

Figure 6-1(c) SYSCON Utility: File Server Information Screen

Chapter 6: Setting Up Users and Groups

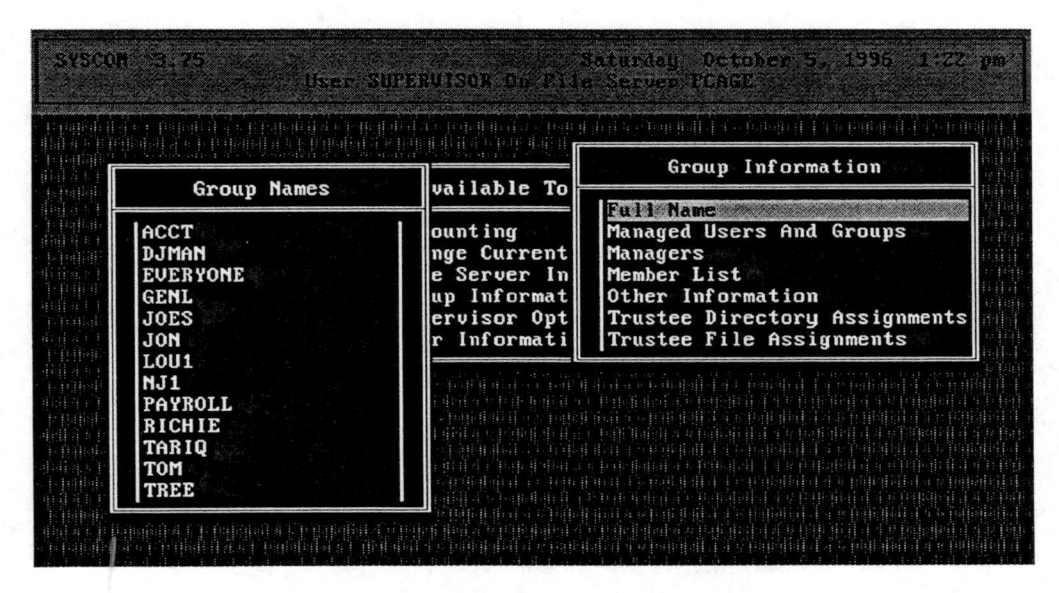

Figure 6-1(d) SYSCON Utility: Group Information Menu

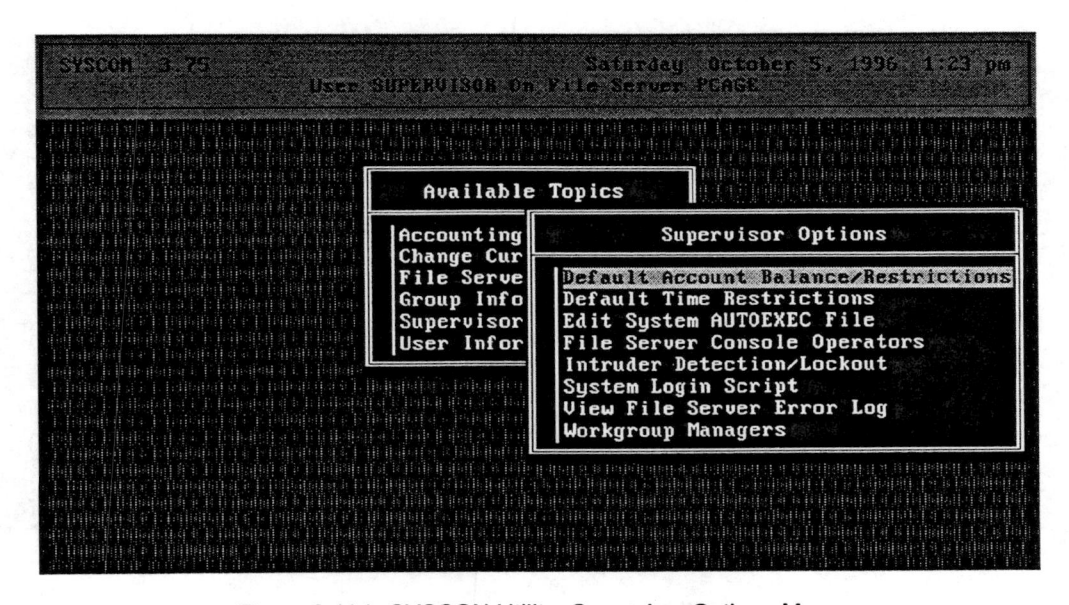

Figure 6-1(e) SYSCON Utility: Supervisor Options Menu

System Administration NetWare 3.12

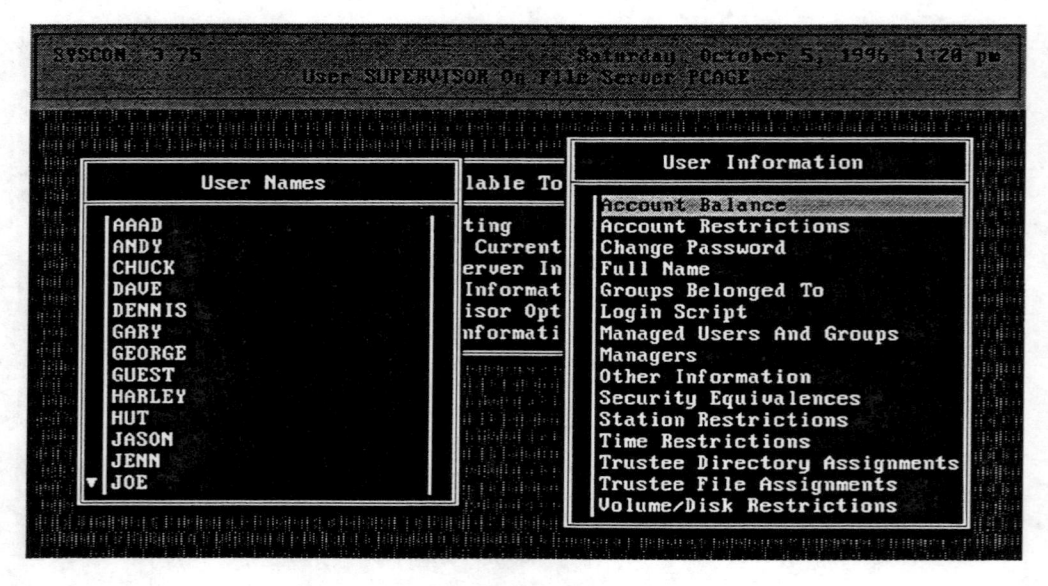

Figure 6-1(f) SYSCON Utility: User Information Menu

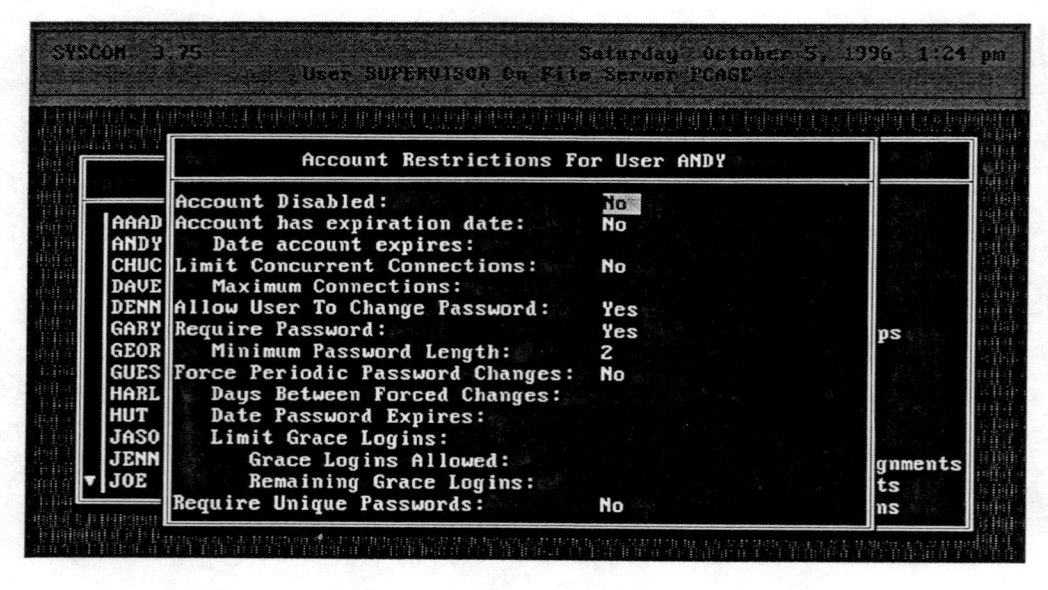

Figure 6-1(g) SYSCON Utility: Account Restrictions Screen

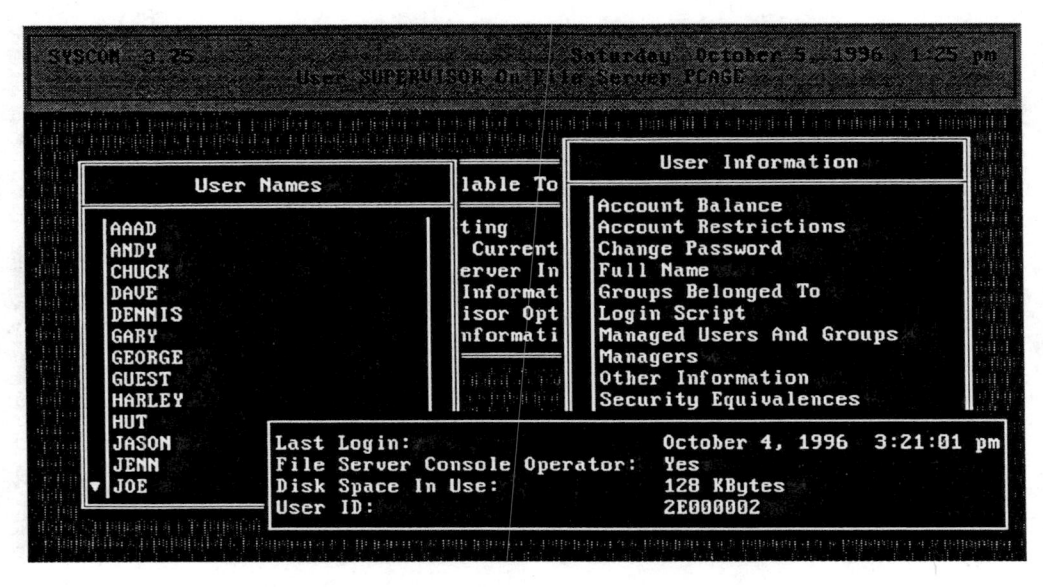

Figure 6-1(h) SYSCON Utility: Other Information Screen

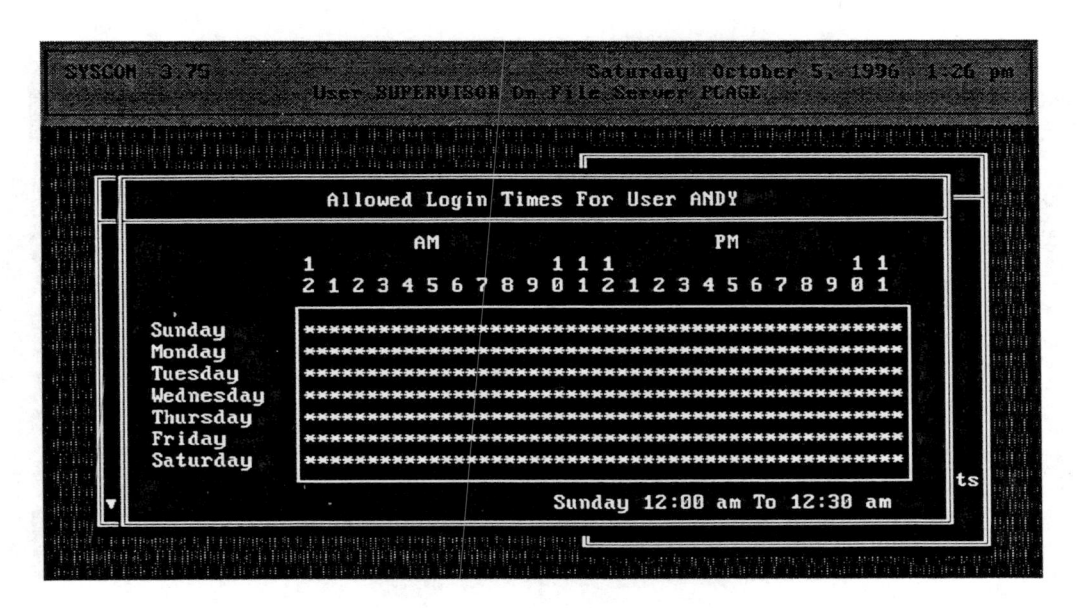

Figure 6-1(i) SYSCON Utility: Time Restrictions Screen

System Administration NetWare 3.12

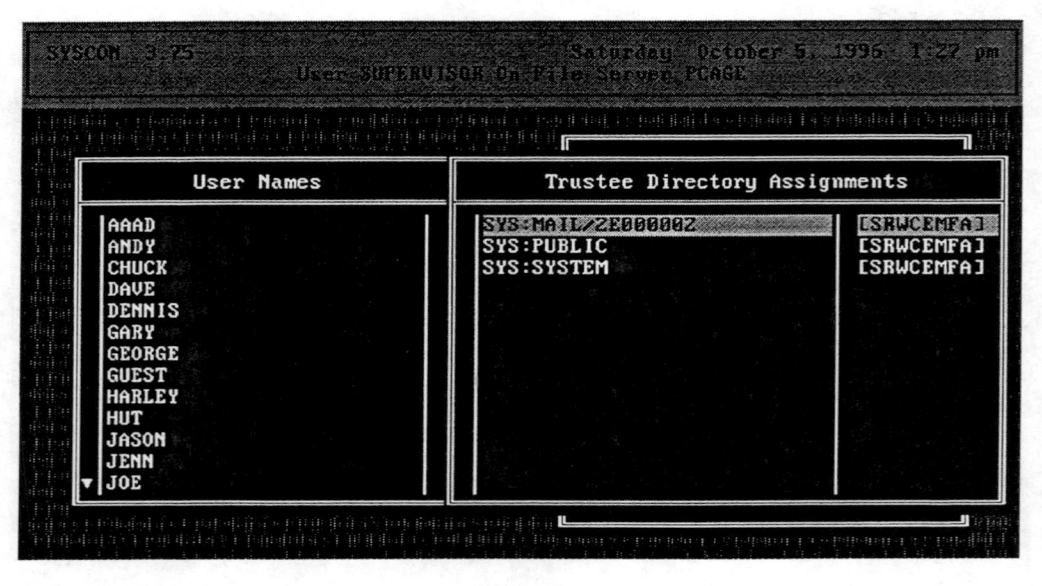

Figure 6-1(j) SYSCON Utility: Trustee Directory Assignments Screen

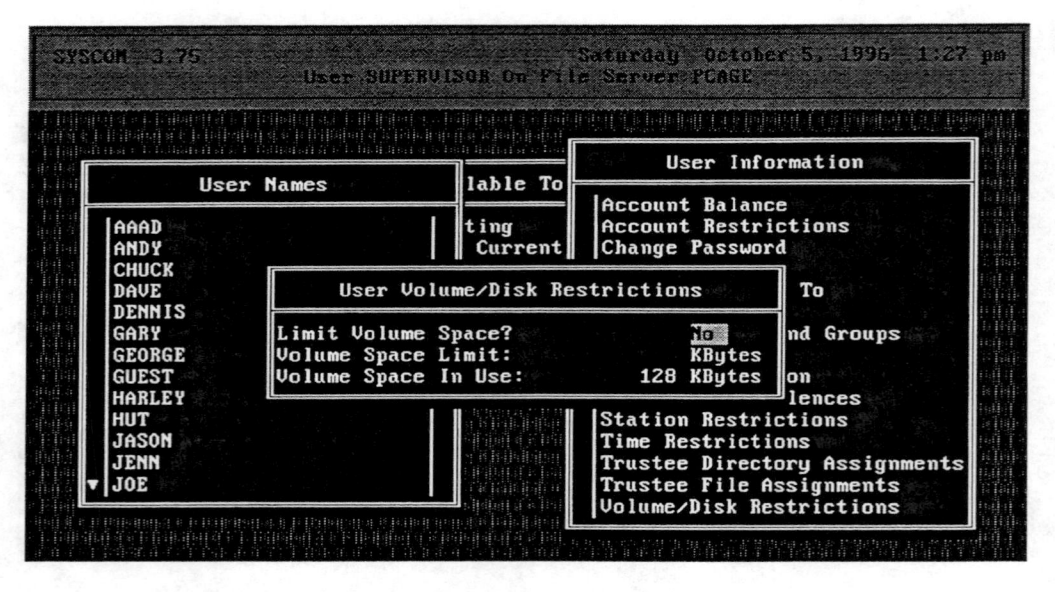

Figure 6-1(k) SYSCON Utility: Volume/Disk Restrictions Screen

MAKEUSER and USERDEF

Both of these utilities can be used to create users. They cannot be used to create groups or to modify existing user accounts.

MAKEUSER

MAKEUSER simplifies the task of creating and deleting multiple users. Using MAKEUSER we first create .USR files containing specific keywords with predefined functions. Then these files are processed to accomplish the actual creation/deletion of users.

Using MAKEUSER you can assign trustee rights to directories. It does not support the creation of trustee file assignments (SYSCON must be used for this).

Available Options
Create New USR File
Edit USR File
Process USR File

Figure 6-2 The MAKEUSER Utility.

MAKEUSER keywords

The keywords you use in MAKEUSER are listed below:

#ACCOUNT_EXPIRATION
#ACCOUNTING
#CLEAR or #RESET
#CONNECTIONS
#CREATE
#DELETE
#GROUP
#HOME_DIRECTORY
#LOGIN_SCRIPT
#MAX_DISK_SPACE
#NO_HOME_DIRECTORY
#PASSWORD_LENGTH
#PASSWORD_PERIOD
#PASSWORD_REQUIRED
#PURGE_USER_DIRECTORY
#REM or REM
#RESTRICTED_TIME
#STATIONS
#UNIQUE_PASSWORD

[handwritten notes: ^ = Create w/o anymore question; ; = Bypass a field]

#ACCOUNT_EXPIRATION *month day year*

Use this keyword to specify when users' accounts expire. If it is not used, the accounts will not expire. Use this keyword only in conjunction with #ACCOUNTING.

Example:

    #account_expiration December 31, 1995

    #create user1^

    #create user2^

#ACCOUNTING balance, lowlimit

Use this keyword to specify the account balance and low balance limit for the users you create. You must have the accounting feature installed on your file server to use this keyword.

Example:

    #accounting 1500, -100

    #create user1

    #clear

    #accounting 1000, 0

    #create user2^

#CLEAR or #RESET

Use these keywords to start a new set of keywords in the same .USR file. All previous keywords encountered in the .USR file have no effect on what follows #CLEAR or #RESET.

Example:

>   #groups sales
>   #create user1^
>   #create user2^
>   #clear
>   #restricted_time sun, 12:00 p.m., 5:00 p.m.
>   #create user3^

#CONNECTIONS *number*

Use this keyword to specify the maximum concurrent connections each user can have. If no number is specified, each user can have as many concurrent connections as the file server supports.

Example:

>   #connections 1
>   #create user1^
>   #create user2^

#CREATE username [;fullname] [;password] [;group] [;directory [rights]]

Use this keyword to create users and specify information about them. You must include *username*; other variables are optional. If more than one group is specified, commas are used to separate them. Commas also separate each directory [rights] sequence.

 # CREATE NAME^ = # CREATE NAME ;;;;

Chapter 6: Setting Up Users and Groups

Example:

#create Bob;Bob Mazzo; pianist;+group1, group2; + SYS:APPS ALL, SYS:DATA ALL

(handwritten annotation: ASSIGNS RIGHTS — pointing to the "+")

The above example creates a user Bob with full name Bob Mazzo; assigns him a password "Pianist"; adds him to groups group1 and group2; and gives him all rights (except Supervisory) in the APPS and DATA directories.

#DELETE username [;username]

Use this keyword to delete users and any information relative to those users. You can enter #DELETE in the same file as #CREATE. If you want to delete the user's home directory when you delete the user, you must precede the DELETE keywords with both HOME_DIRECTORY and PURGE_USER_DIRECTORY.

Example:

> #home_directory SYS:USERS
>
> #create bob^
>
> #create mike^
>
> #create alex^
>
> #purge_user_directory
>
> #delete alba; george; john

#GROUP group [;group]

Use this keyword to assign users to groups. Only groups you have already created with SYSCON can be included.

© 1993 - 95 · PC Age, Inc. All Rights Reserved · 20 Audrey Place · Fairfield, NJ 07004 · U.S.A. · Tel: 201-882-5370

Example:

   #groups wp;dbase

   #create mike^

#HOME_DIRECTORY *path*

Use this keyword to assign or delete a home directory when creating or deleting a user.

Example:

   #home_directory sys:newusers

   #purge_user_directory

   #delete james^

#LOGIN_SCRIPT *path*

Use this keyword to specify the location of the file containing a login script to be copied and used as each new user's login script. MAKEUSER places the file in each user's mail. The file containing the login script must already exist.

Example:

   #login_script sys:public/everyone.log

   #create mike^

#MAX_DISK_SPACE vol, number [;vol, number]

Use this keyword to specify the maximum number of disk blocks (4KB in size) allocated per volume for each new user. Use this keyword only if the volume limitation option was set with DSPACE.

Example:

   #max_disk_space SYS, 1024

   #create charles^

#NO_HOME_DIRECTORY

Use this keyword to specify that a user home directory not be created.

#PASSWORD_LENGTH *length*

Use this keyword to specify the minimum length of the new user's passwords. Replace *length* with a number between 1 to 20. The default is five characters. You must enter PASSWORD_REQUIRED before you enter PASSWORD_LENGTH.

Example:

   #password_required

   #password_length 5

   #create bob^

#PASSWORD_PERIOD *days*

Use this keyword to assign the number of days between password expirations. You must enter PASSWORD_REQUIRED before you enter PASSWORD_PERIOD.

Example:

#password_required

#password_period 30

#create mike^

#PASSWORD_REQUIRED

Use this keyword to require users to have a password.

Example:

#password_required

#create bob;;apple^

#PURGE_USER_DIRECTORY

Use this keyword to delete any subdirectories owned by the user when the user is deleted. Use it also in conjunction with the HOME_DIRECTORY keyword to delete the user's home directory. You must enter this keyword before #DELETE. If you want to delete the user's home directory, you must include #HOME_DIRECTORY.

Example:

#home_directory SYS:USERS

#purge_user_directory

#delete mike^

#REM or REM

Use this keyword to make comments about the information in your .USR file.

Example:

#rem students in CNE course group October 1993

#create student1^

#create student2^

#create student3^

#RESTRICTED_TIME day, start, end [;day, start, end]

Use this keyword to specify which days and hours new users cannot login to the file server.

Example:

#restricted_time sat, 12:00 a.m., 11:59 p.m.;sun, 12:00 a.m., 11:59 p.m.

#create mike^

#STATIONS network, station [;station] [;network, station]

Use this keyword to specify the physical workstations from which users can login to the file server. The hexadecimal network address cannot exceed 8 digits. The hexadecimal station address cannot have more than 11 digits. If all stations are to be included for any given network, you can replace the station address with "all" (e.g., "Stations AAA1, all").

Example:

   #station AAA1, AB, CD

   #create alba^

#UNIQUE_PASSWORD

Use this keyword to prevent users from reusing any of their previous 8 passwords when they change their passwords. You must enter PASSWORD_REQUIRED before you enter UNIQUE_PASSWORD.

Example:

   #password_required

   #password_period 15

   #unique_password

   #create mike^

*[handwritten: APPEND ↓ NDIR *.* > ~ G:\USERS\JOHN\TEST]*

USERDEF

This utility is used to create multiple users with similar characteristics. When creating users with USERDEF, we can also set up basic login scripts, specify home directories, establish print job configurations, assign account and disk space restrictions, and set minimal login and password security.

To use USERDEF to create multiple users, we need to do the following:

1. Do some preliminary work before using the USERDEF. For example, install the accounting options in SYSCON and set the print environment in the PRINTCON and PRINTDEF utilities (create print job configurations, etc.). Create the directory USERS for a users' home directory.

2. Run USERDEF and choose the "Add Users" option from the "Available Options" menu.

3. Choose the default or custom template from the "Templates" list.

Now you can create new users by pressing the <Ins> key. Enter the user's full name and then the login name. Repeat this step for each user you create with the selected template. When you are done, press <Esc> and follow USERDEF's prompts to create the new users you have just defined.

```
┌─────────────────────────────────────────────────────────┐
│  USERDEF  3.53              Friday  October 8, 1993  4:17 pm │
│           User SUPERVISOR On File Server  PCAGE         │
└─────────────────────────────────────────────────────────┘

            ┌─────────────────────────────┐
            │      Available Options      │
            ├─────────────────────────────┤
            │  Add Users                  │
            │  Edit/View Templates        │
            │  Restrict User              │
            └─────────────────────────────┘

    ┌─────────────────────────────────────────────────┐
    │       Login Script For Template DEFAULT         │
    ├─────────────────────────────────────────────────┤
    │  map  s1:=sys:public                            │
    │  map  s2 :=sys:public\%machine\%os\%os_version  │
    │  comspec = s2:command.com                       │
    │  map *1 :=%default_directory\%login_name        │
    └─────────────────────────────────────────────────┘

        ┌─────────────────────────────────────────────┐
        │       Parameters For Template DEFAULT       │
        ├─────────────────────────────────────────────┤
        │  Default Directory:   SYS:                  │
        │  Copy PrintCon From:   (see list)           │
        │  Group Belonged To:    (see list)           │
        │  Account Balance:              1000         │
        │  Limit Account Balance:        No           │
        │       Low Limit:                       0    │
        │  Limit Concurrent Connections: No           │
        │       Maximum Connections:     8            │
        │                                             │
        │  Require Password:             Yes          │
        │       Minimum Password Length:    5         │
        │  Force Periodic Password Changes: Yes       │
        │       Days Between Forced Changes: 90       │
        │  Require Unique Passwords:     Yes          │
        └─────────────────────────────────────────────┘
```

Figure 6-3 The USERDEF Utility.

Review Questions

Q.1. A workgroup manager cannot _____ . (select all that are true)

    a. create users

    b. delete the users he created

    c. delete the users supervisor created

    d. assign trustee rights to the users he is managing

Q.2. A console operator cannot _____ .

    a. broadcast message   b. enable or disable login

    c. clear connections   d. change system date and time

Q.3. Which of the following utility would you use to create users and install accounting?

    a. SYSCON   b. MAKEUSER

    c. USERDEF   d. SYSACCT

Q.4. In which of the following utilities do you use KEYWORDS to create users?

    a. SYSCON   b. MAKEUSER
    c. USERDEF   d. USERS

Q.5. In which of the following utilities do you use a TEMPLATE to create users?

    a. SYSCON   b. MAKEUSER
    c. USERDEF   d. USERS

Q.6. Which one of the following utilities can be used to make trustee file assignments?

    a. SYSCON   b. MAKEUSER
    c. USERDEF   d. USERS

Q.7. Files created with MAKEUSER have the extension _____ .

    a. USR   b. DAT
    c. SRC   d. MAK

Q.8. Which of the utilities allow you to specify a login script for the user?

    a. SYSCON   b. MAKEUSER

    c. USERDEF   d. All of these utilities

Chapter 7   Security

Security Levels

NetWare provides very high levels of security and access control. The system keeps a security profile of each user and only allows access to directories at which security levels have been assigned by the system Supervisor. NetWare provides three basic types of security:

- Login/Password Restrictions
- Rights Security
- Attribute Security

Login/Password Restrictions

To allow a user to use a network, a user account must be created for that user. A password may also be required for security purposes. A password can have the following options:

- Minimum password length
- Periodic password change
- Unique password
- Grace logins after password expiration

The supervisor who sets up the user can also specify the minimum length of the user's password, how often the password should be changed, etc. The password length limitation prevents users from using short passwords that are easy to guess. Five or six characters is a reasonable length for password. We can view a user's password restrictions by selecting that user in the SYSCON utility.

Periodic password changes force users to change their passwords after a specific number of days, typically 30 to 60. The passwords for organizations that have highly confidential data should be changed frequently.

The unique password feature prevents users from using the same password over and over again.

The limited "grace" login feature lets users continue to use their password for a limited number of times after it has expired. The system reduces the limited grace number by one after each reminder to the user. If this number reaches zero, the system locks out that user's account.

Station, Time, and Other Account Restrictions

These features are optional and configurable to meet the needs of different networks.

Station Restriction

This feature restricts the user to login from only that network and stations whose addresses have been assigned to him. He cannot login from any other station.

Time Restriction

This feature lets users login only during specified days and hours. For example, we can restrict users from logging in on weekends and after office hours.

Other restrictions include the number of concurrent connections a user can have and the maximum number of failed password attempts (intruder limits). Intruder limits help prevent intruders from guessing passwords.

Setting Default Account Restrictions

Default account restrictions can be set with the SYSCON utility under Supervisor Options for new users. These default restrictions will be applied to newly created users (not to existing users).

Rights Security

"**Rights**" control which directories and files a user or group can access and what the user or group is allowed to do with those directories and files. NetWare 3.12 features eight different rights, each of which is identified by its first initial.

NetWare 3.12 Rights

Identity Initial	Right Name	Function
S	Supervisory	Gives the user all rights in the directory, its files, and its subdirectories. Once assigned to the user in a parent directory, this right cannot be filtered out by the IRM in subdirectories or files. If added to the IRM, it then cannot be deleted.
R	Read	Allows a user to read a file.
W	Write	Allows a user to write or modify a file.
C	Create	Allows the user to create files and subdirectories in the directory.
E	Erase	Allows the user to delete files and subdirectories in a directory.
M	Modify	Allows the user to rename or change the attributes of the directory, its files and subdirectories.
F	File Scan	Allows the user to see the directory's files in a directory listing.
A	Access Control	Allows the user to change trustee assignments and the IRM for the directory, subdirectories and files. The user who has the Access Control right can grant any right (except Supervisory) to other users or to himself.

The Supervisor has all rights in all directories and grants trustee assignments to users and groups. The group EVERYONE has the following default rights:

- Create in SYS:MAIL
- Read and File Scan in SYS:PUBLIC
- Read and File Scan in SYS:LOGIN

Rights Requirements

The rights required to complete common tasks are listed below:

Task	Rights
See a file name or subdirectory	F
Search a directory for files	F
Read from a closed file (usually granted with the right to see file name)	R
Copy files to a directory	W, C, F
Copy files from a directory	F, R
Create and write to a file	C
Execute a file	F, R
Write to a closed file (usually granted with the right to see the file name)	W,C,E,M
Change file or directory attributes	M
Rename a file or directory	M
Delete a file or directory	E
Change trustee assignments	A
Change the Inherited Rights Mask	A

Note: The above rights are for the NetWare NCOPY command. The DOS copy command has different requirements:

Copy from a directory   R

Copy to a directory   C

Trustee Rights Assignments

When a Supervisor assigns rights to a user or group, the user or group becomes a "trustee" of that particular directory or file. Therefore these rights are known as **Trustee Rights**.

In NetWare 3.1x, users and groups can have rights specified down to the file level. If rights are not specifically changed for a file, users will have the access level provided by the directory rights that have been granted.

The SYSCON menu utility and the GRANT, REMOVE, and REVOKE commands may be used for setting user and group rights.

The Inherited Rights Mask (IRM)

The Inherited Rights Mask determines what rights a user can inherit from the parent directory. A user can inherit only those rights from a parent directory that the user has in that directory. A user cannot inherit rights from a directory that he has not been granted.

By default, the IRM contains the full set of NetWare rights. If we want to prevent certain rights from being inherited from a parent directory, we must remove those from the child directory's IRM.

We can use either FILER or the ALLOW utility to modify the IRM. The **Access Control** right is a must to modify an IRM.

Effective Rights

A user's effective rights are those rights the user can actually exercise in a given directory or file. Effective rights are determined by looking at the combination of trustee right assignments and the IRM. Effective rights are determined by trustee assignments, if they exist. Otherwise, the effective rights of the current directory are determined by the intersection of the effective rights of the parent directory and the current directory's IRM. Trustee assignments override the directory's IRM.

Calculating Effective Rights

The following three rules can be used to determine a user's effective rights:

1. Add together all the rights granted to the user through direct trustee assignments, through a group membership, and through security equivalence for the file and directory. These are user's total effective rights.

    However, when there are explicit rights assignments, no rights can be inherited. See also rule 3.

2. If the user does not have any directly granted rights, including through group membership and security equivalence, combine all inherited rights. Then subtract any rights blocked by an IRM.

3. If the user is granted rights directly but not through a group membership, it can inherit rights granted as a group membership from higher level (as allowed by the IRM), but cannot inherit rights granted directly (as a user) at the higher level. See Example 7-2 for more explanation.

Example 7-1

APPS	IRM	[S R W C E M F A]
	Inherited Rights	[- - - - - - - -]
	Explicit User Trustee Assignment	[- R - C E - F -]
	Effective Rights	[- R - C E - F -]
APPS\WP	IRM	[S - - R - - F -]
	Inherited Rights[1]	[- - - - - - - -]
	Explicit User Trustee Assignment[2]	[- - - C E - F -]
	Effective Rights	[- - - C E - F -]
APPS\WP\DOC	IRM	[S - - C E - F -]
	Inherited Rights	[- - - - E - F -]
	Explicit User Trustee Assignment	[- - - - - - - -]
	Effective Rights	[- - - - E - F -]
APPS\WP\DOC\FILE1	IRM	[- R - C E - F -]
	Inherited Rights	[- - - - - - - -]
	Explicit User Trustee Assignment	[- R - C - - F -]
	Effective Rights	[- R - C - - F -]

1. User cannot inherit any rights from a parent directory when there are explicit trustee assignments.
2. From this point, user can only inherit trustee rights granted here if there are no explicit trustee assignments (at lower level).

Example 7-2

APPS	IRM	[S R W C E M F A]
	Inherited Rights	[- - - - - - - -]
	Explicit User Trustee Assignment	[- - - - E - F -]
	Explicit Group Trustee Assignment	[- R - C - - - -]
	Effective Rights	[- R - C E - F -]
APPS\WP	IRM	[S R - C - - - -]
	Inherited Rights (User and group rights[1])	[- R - C - - - -]
	Explicit User Trustee Assignment	[- - - - - - - -]
	Explicit Group Trustee Assignment	[- - - - - - - -]
	Effective Rights	[- R - C - - - -]
APPS\WP\DOC	IRM	[S - - C E - F -]
	Inherited Rights (group rights[2])	[- - - C - - - -]
	Explicit User Trustee Assignment	[- - - - - - F -]
	Explicit Group Trustee Assignment	[- - - - - - - -]
	Effective Rights	[- - - C - - F -]
APPS\WP\DOC\FILE1	IRM	[S R - - - - F -]
	Inherited Rights (User rights[3])	[- - - - - - F -]
	Explicit User Trustee Assignment	[- - - - - - - -]
	Explicit Group Trustee Assignment	[- - - C - - - -]
	Effective Rights	[- - - C - - F -]

1. When you do not grant rights as a user and group, user and group rights can be inherited from the parent directory.

2. When you explicitly grant user rights, user rights cannot be inherited from the parent directory, but group rights can be inherited (if you do not grant group rights).

3. When you explicitly grant group rights, group rights cannot be inherited from the parent directory, but user rights can be inherited (if you do not grant user rights).

Exercise 7.1

Find out the effective rights of a user in APPS, APPS\WP, APPS\WP\DOC, and APPS\WP\DOC\FILE1.

Rights	S	R	W	C	E	M	F	A
Explicit Trustee rights granted in APPS as a user		X					X	
Explicit Trustee rights granted in APPS as a member of a group			X	X				
Effective rights in APPS								
IRM of APPS\WP	S	R	W	C	E	M	F	A
Explicit Trustee rights granted in APPS\WP as a user					X	X		
Effective rights in APPS\WP								
IRM of APPS\WP\DOC	S	R		C		M	F	A
Effective rights in APPS\WP\DOC								
IRM of FILE1 in DOC directory	S	R					F	
Explicit Trustee rights granted for FILE1 in DOC directory as a user		X					X	
Effective rights in APPS\WP\DOC\FILE1								

Figure 7-1 Calculation of Effective Rights.

Attribute Security

Attributes are special properties of files and directories that prevent tasks that rights would otherwise allow. Attributes apply equally to the user Supervisor and users with the supervisory right. If a user has the Modify right, he can change the attributes also.

NetWare 3.12 has two categories of attributes:

- Directory Attributes
- File Attributes

File and Directory Attributes

We can assign attributes to files and directories in FILER or by using the FLAG utility (for files) and the FLAGDIR utility (for directories and volumes). To do this, we must have the modify right in the directory.

Attribute	Identity Initial(s)	Description
Hidden	H*	Hides directories and files from DOS DIR scan. NDIR will show the hidden directories and files to a user with the File Scan right. This attribute prevents directories or files from being deleted or copied.
System	Sy*	Hides directories and files from DOS DIR scan. NDIR will show the hidden directories or files to a user with the File Scan right. This attribute prevents the directory or files from being deleted or copied. Assign to system files and their directories.
Delete Inhibit	D*	Protects the directory or files from being deleted. Users cannot delete the directory or file even if they have the Erase right. Users with the Modify right could remove the Delete Inhibit attribute and then delete the directory or file.

Attribute	Identity Initial(s)	Description
Rename Inhibit	R*	User cannot rename the directory or file when this attribute is assigned. Users with the Modify right could remove the Rename Inhibit attribute and then rename the directory or file.
Read Only	Ro	Users cannot write to, change, erase, or rename the file even if they have Write and Erase rights.
Read Write	Rw	Allows users to modify a file.
Shareable	S	Allows several users to use a file simultaneously. Application program files should be Shareable and Read Only.
Copy Inhibit	C	Applies to Macintosh workstations. Prevents Mac users from copying the file.
Execute Only	X	Prevents files from being copied or backed up. This attribute cannot be removed once granted.
Normal	N*	Use Normal to clear all attributes. The default is Rw.
ALL	ALL	Use to set all attributes.

Note: You can use the /SUB option with the FLAG command to view or change file attributes in directories and their subdirectories.

Attributes with * can be used with both files and directories.

Other Attributes

NetWare 3.12 uses other attributes that are not security-related.

Attribute	Identity Initial(s)	Description
Archive Needed	A	This attribute is automatically assigned when a file is created or modified.
Purge	P*	Causes NetWare to immediately purge the file when it is deleted. When assigned to a directory, all files in the directory will be purged when they are deleted.
Transactional	T	Protects files by NetWare's Transaction Tracking System (TTS). Should be assigned to database files.
Indexed	I	Use this attribute for faster access of the file. (Assigned automatically to files with over 64 FAT entries).
Read Audit	Ra	NetWare does not currently use this attribute.
Write Audit	Wa	-same as above-

Note: Attributes with * can be used with both files and directories.

File Server Security

The file server security features of NetWare control access to the file server console. For tight control, only the Supervisor and Console Operator should be able to use the console. Only the Supervisor and equivalent should have rights in the SYS:SYSTEM directory. The MONITOR (lock feature) and SECURE CONSOLE utilities should be used to prevent unauthorized access to the console.

[handwritten annotation: Removes Command.com from memory]

The NetWare Bindery

NetWare stores the security information about users, groups and other objects in a database called the bindery. The bindery has three components:

- **Object:** A user, group, print server, file server, or any other entity that has been given a name. NetWare assigns a unique ID number for each bindery object.

- **Properties:** The characteristics associated with bindery object. Examples include passwords, account restrictions, account balances, groups the user belongs to, etc.

- **Data Sets:** Values assigned to the bindery object's properties.

In NetWare 3.12, the bindery is made up of three separate files located in the SYS:SYSTEM directory.

- NET$OBJ.SYS contains object information.
- NET$PROP.SYS contains property information.
- NET$VAL.SYS contains property values.

Using Security-Related NetWare Commands

ALLOW

Use ALLOW to view, set, or modify the Inherited Rights Mask (IRM) of a directory or file. You can specify ALL for all eight rights or specify rights individually (separated by a space).

Examples:

    ALLOW SYS:APPS\WP\DOC F R W E M C
    ALLOW G: ALL

GRANT

Use GRANT to grant trustee rights to users or groups in a file or directory. You can specify ALL for all eight rights or specify rights individually (separated by a space).

Examples:

    GRANT R F TO USER BOB
    GRANT ALL FOR G: TO MIKE

REVOKE

Use REVOKE to revoke trustee rights from a user or group in a file or directory.

Examples:

> REVOKE ALL FROM BOB
>
> REVOKE A M E FOR SYS:APPS FROM MIKE

REMOVE

Use REMOVE to delete a user or group from the trustee list of a file or a directory.

Examples:

> REMOVE USER BOB FROM SYS:APPS\WP
>
> REMOVE GROUP SALES FROM G:

FLAG

Use FLAG to view or change the attributes of files in a given directory.

Examples:

> FLAG *.EXE RO S
>
> FLAG *.* N

FLAGDIR

Use FLAGDIR to view or change the attributes of subdirectories or volumes.

Examples:

    FLAGDIR * P

    FLAGDIR WP P D

    FLAGDIR SYS:

TLIST

Use TLIST to view the trustee list of a file or a directory. The user must have the Access Control right in a directory to view the trustee list of that directory or its files.

RIGHTS

Use RIGHTS to view your effective rights in a file or a directory.

For more explanation of the above commands, check the Novell *Utilities Reference* manual.

NCP Packet Signature

NCP Packet Signature is an enhanced security feature that protects servers and clients using the NCP (NetWare Core Protocol) by preventing packet forgery.

Without NCP packet signature, a client can pose as another client and get privileged services from the file server.

NCP packet signature is installed when a client logs in to a NetWare 3.12 server. Both server and client determine a unique key (also referred to as the session key) and use this key with

each packet (it is called signing the packet or packet signature). The packet signature changes with every packet.
When a server receives a request from a client, it checks the packet signature for that particular client. If it is correct, the server processes the request and attaches a new signature to the reply.

NCP packets with incorrect signatures are discarded and an alert message is sent to the server console and to the server error log file.

Because the packet signature process affects the performance, it is optional for the client and for the server. Several signature levels are available to provide no signature security to maximum signature security.

Server Levels

Server packet signature levels are assigned by a new SET parameter.

SET NCP PACKET SIGNATURE OPTION=*number*

Supported Values: 0, 1, 2, or 3.

Default: 1.

Number	Explanation
0	Server does not sign packets (regardless of the workstation level)
1	Server signs packets only if the workstation requests it (workstation level is 1 or higher)
2	Server signs packets if the workstation is capable of signing (workstation level is 1 or higher)
3	Server signs packets and requires all workstations to sign packets (or login will fail)

Workstation Levels

Workstation signature levels are assigned by a new NET.CFG parameter under the NetWare DOS Requester section heading:

SIGNATURE LEVEL=*number*

Supported Values: 0, 1, 2, or 3.

Default: 1

Number	Explanation
0	Workstation does not sign packets.
1	Workstation signs packets only if the server requests it server option is 2 or higher)
2	Workstation signs packets if the server is capable of signing (server option is 1 or higher)
3	Workstation signs packets and requires the server to sign packets (or login will fail)

Effective Packet Signature of Server and Workstation

IF	Server=0	Server=1	Server=2	Server=3
Workstation=0	No packet signature	No packet signature	No packet signature	Login fails
Workstation=1	No packet signature	No packet signature *	Packet signature	Packet signature
Workstation=2	No packet signature	Packet signature	Packet signature	Packet signature
Workstation=3	Login fails	Packet signature	Packet signature	Packet signature**

* Default Setting
** Maximum Security

Figure 7-2 Effective Packet Signature

If you have very sensitive data on the server, you may want to set the server to level 3 and all workstations to level 3 for maximum protection.

If you have sensitive data in only some separate directories, you may set the server level to 2 and the workstations that need to access the sensitive data to level 3. All other workstations may be at the default level 1.

If employees can use any workstation on the network and the server has some sensitive data, you may set the server level to 3 and workstation at the default level 1.

If your network is accessed by an unattended workstation for non-sensitive information and you have sensitive data on some servers, set the server with sensitive data to level 3 and the unattended workstation to level 0.

Answer to Exercise 7.1

Rights	S	R	W	C	E	M	F	A
Explicit Trustee rights granted in APPS as a user		X					X	
Explicit Trustee rights granted in APPS as a member of a group			X	X				
Effective rights in APPS		X	X	X			X	
IRM of APPS\WP	S	R	W	C	E	M	F	A
Explicit Trustee rights granted in APPS\WP as a user					X	X		
Effective rights in APPS\WP			X	X	X	X		
IRM of APPS\WP\DOC	S	R		C		M	F	A
Effective rights in APPS\WP\DOC				X		X		
IRM of FILE1 in DOC directory	S	R					F	
Explicit Trustee rights granted for FILE1 in DOC directory as a user		X					X	
Effective rights in APPS\WP\DOC\FILE1		X					X	

Review Questions

Q.1. The unique password feature prevents _____ .

    a. a user using the same password used by other user
    b. a user using the same password again
    c. a user using the password fewer then 5 characters
    d. a user using a unique password

Q.2. A user can execute a file if he has which of the following rights? (select all that are true)

    a. S   b. A
    c. RF   d. R

Q.3. If a user has R and F rights in APPS directory, and he is given the trustee rights C and W in the APPS\WP directory. What rights, will he have in the APPS\WP\DOC directory?

    a. R, F   b. R, F, C, W
    c. C, W   d. none

Q.4. How would you modify an IRM?

    a. by deleting rights

    b. by adding rights

    c. by assigning trustee rights

    d. by using GRANT utility

Q.5. A supervisor can delete a file if the file is Read-Only.

    a. true   b. false

    c. after changing the attribute   d. if using FILER utility

Q.6. Which of the following files stores user names?

    a. SYSCON   b. NET$OBJ.SYS

    c. NET$VAL.SYS   d. USERS

Q.7. Which of the following commands can be used to delete a user from the trustee list of directory?

    a. REVOKE   b. REMOVE

    c. DELETE   d. ALLOW

Q.8. Which of the following is not a correct way to revoke trustee rights from a user in a directory?

    a. REVOKE ALL FROM BOB

    b. REVOKE ALL FROM BOB FOR SYS:APPS

    c. REVOKE RF FROM USER BOB

    d. REVOKE AMF FOR SYS:APPS FROM BOB

Q.9. If a user has supervisory right in SYS volume, he can create users.

    a. true   b. false

Q.10. To change file attributes in the current directory and subdirectories, which command would you use?

    a. FLAG *.* RO /S   b. FLAG *.* RO /SUB

    c. FLAG *.* RO /ALL   d. FLAG FOR ALL RO

Q.11. When you create a new file on a network, which attributes the file has by default?

    a. Read Only, Sharable, Archive Needed

    b. Read Only, Non-Shareable, Archive Needed

    c. Read Write, Sharable

    d. Read Write, Non-Shareable, Archive Needed

Chapter 8 Managing the Workstation Connection

Connecting a Workstation

To convert a stand-alone PC into a network workstation, we first plug a network interface card (NIC) into the PC's expansion bus (available slot). We then connect a cable to the NIC, giving the PC a physical connection to the network.

After hardware connections, we need the following workstation software to get services from the network:

- NetWare DOS Requester
- Communication Protocol

NetWare DOS Requester

NetWare DOS Requester provides an interface between the local DOS applications and the NetWare operating system. If any requests from the user or programs require network access (NetWare services), the DOS Requester converts these requests to NCP (NetWare Core Protocol) packets and then hands them to IPX (NetWare Communication Protocol) for transmission. The

DOS Requester replaces the NetWare Shell (NETx) which is used in previous versions of NetWare.

The NetWare DOS Requester is composed of many files called Virtual Loadable Modules (VLMs) that can be loaded and unloaded as needed.

To load NetWare DOS Requester into workstation memory, we run VLM.EXE. When VLM.EXE is executed, it loads the VLMs from the current directory or another specified directory. A directory can be specified at execution or in the NET.CFG (NetWare workstation Configuration) file.

Like older NetWare Shells (NETx, XMSNETx, EMSNETx), NetWare can be loaded in conventional, extended, or expanded memory.

Examples:

Command	Description
C:>VLM <enter>	Loads the DOS Requester (VLMs) found in the current directory or as specified in NET.CFG.
C:>VLM /c=path	Loads the DOS Requester using VLMs found in the directory specified by path.
C:>VLM /mc	Loads the DOS Requester in conventional memory.
C:>VLM /mx	Loads the DOS Requester in extended memory.
C:>VLM /me	Loads the DOS Requester in expanded memory.

Communication Protocol

After the DOS Requester has built the NCP packets, it needs a communication protocol to transmit these packets.

Protocol is simply the rules or conventions for communication. If two systems want to communicate, they must use the same protocol (same language) to understand each other.

IPX (Internetwork Packet eXchange) is the communication protocol used on NetWare networks. IPX passes the packets to the Link Support Layer (LSL), which uses LAN drivers to access the network board for the actual transmission of the packet through the cable.

Open Data-Link Interface (ODI)

ODI supports multiple transport protocols (e.g., IPX/SPX, TCP/IP) in a single workstation or on a single server. ODI allows multiple transport protocols to share the same network board without conflict. For example, ODI provides TCP/IP support, which is traditionally limited to Ethernet, over ARCnet or Token Ring. It means that both IPX and TCP/IP can run on the same workstation using the same board. The ODI specification allows network boards to support different transport protocols (with the help of the MLID (Multiple Link Interface Driver) and the LSL).

Using the ODI specification, NetWare server's services are available to all workstations regardless of the transport protocols they are using. At this level (NetWare Server's Services), this uniform transport interface is provided by the Streams interface — an interface developed by AT&T in UNIX System V.

ODI provides a standard interface for transport protocols by using the following layers:

- Network board and the MLID (Multiple Link Interface Driver) Layer
- Link Support Layer (LSL)
- Protocol Stack Layer

All these layers are used in communication to the NetWare operating system.

The ODI LAN drivers are different from previous drivers. They are called Multiple Link Interface Drivers because they can accept any type of packet, such as IPX, AppleTalk (from Macintosh workstations), or TCP/IP (from UNIX workstations).

The Link Support Layer (LSL) identifies the type of packet it receives and then passes the packet to the appropriate protocol in the protocol stack layer (like a switchboard).

The Protocol Stack Layer contains protocol stacks such as IPX/SPX, AppleTalk, and TCP/IP. When a specified protocol stack receives a packet, it passes it to communicate with NetWare 3.12 or sends it back through the layers to another network.

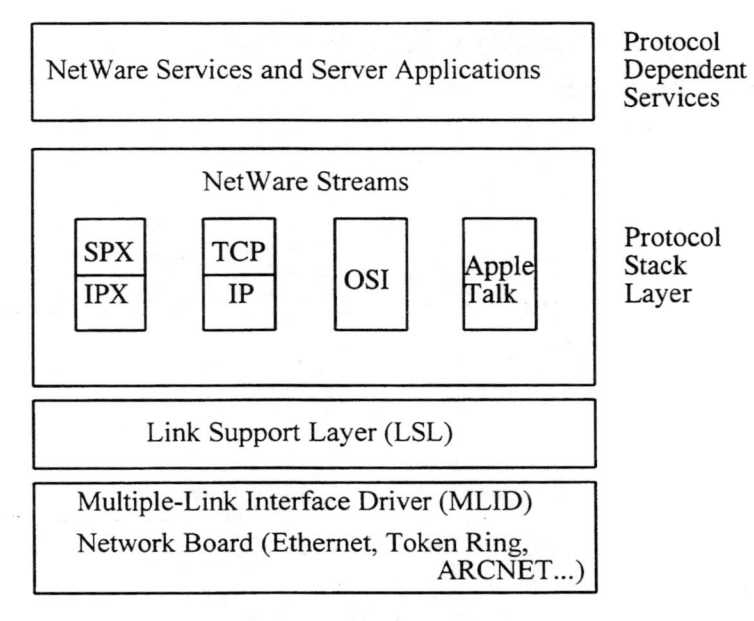

```
                  ┌─────────────────────────────────────┐   Protocol
                  │ NetWare Services and Server Applications │   Dependent
                  └─────────────────────────────────────┘   Services

                  ┌─────────────────────────────────────┐
                  │         NetWare Streams             │
                  │  ┌────┐ ┌────┐ ┌────┐ ┌──────┐     │   Protocol
                  │  │SPX │ │TCP │ │    │ │Apple │     │   Stack
                  │  │IPX │ │IP  │ │OSI │ │Talk  │     │   Layer
                  │  └────┘ └────┘ └────┘ └──────┘     │
                  └─────────────────────────────────────┘

                  ┌─────────────────────────────────────┐
                  │     Link Support Layer (LSL)        │
                  └─────────────────────────────────────┘
                  ┌─────────────────────────────────────┐
                  │ Multiple-Link Interface Driver (MLID) │
                  │ Network Board (Ethernet, Token Ring, │
                  │                          ARCNET...) │
                  └─────────────────────────────────────┘
```

Figure 8-1 Open Data-Link Interface (ODI)

Software to Connect a DOS Workstation

To connect a DOS workstation to a NetWare 3.12 network, boot the workstation with DOS and then load the ODI files in the following order:

    LSL

    NE2000   (or any other MLID)

    IPXODI

    VLM

The client installation process creates a directory C:\NWCLIENT to store these files. A file named STARTNET.BAT is created to load these files. AUTOEXEC.BAT file is modified to call STARTNET.BAT.

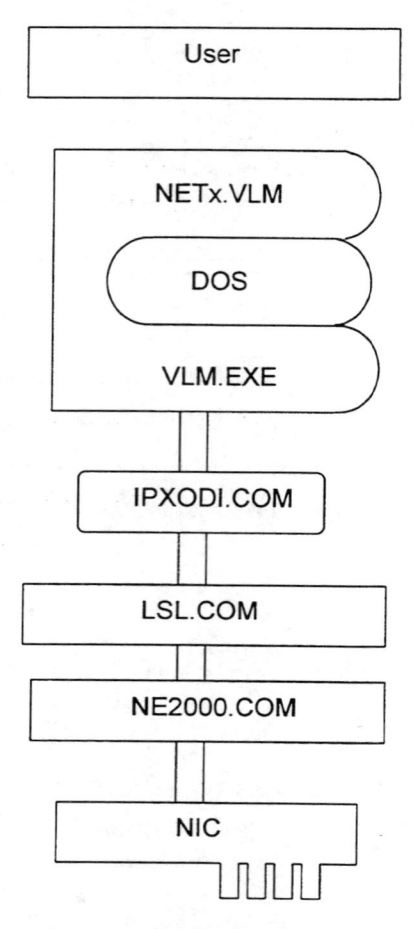

Figure 8-2 ODI Workstation

Workstation Configuration Files

The following three files are used to configure a workstation:

1. CONFIG.SYS
2. AUTOEXEC.BAT
3. NET.CFG

CONFIG.SYS

This is a DOS configuration file. NetWare 3.12 requires the LASTDRIVE command in this file so that the DOS Requester can identify the drive letters available as network drives letters. DOS Requester makes available all letters between the last known physical drive and the letter specified in the LASTDRIVE command.

For example, if the workstation has three local drives A:, B:, and C:, and you specify LASTDRIVE=Z in the CONFIG.SYS file, the letters D through Z will be available for mapping as network drives.

AUTOEXEC.BAT

The AUTOEXEC.BAT file is also a DOS file which is used to automatically execute commands whenever a user boots a workstation. This file can be used to automate the login to the system. The NetWare 3.12 workstation installation program creates a file named STARTNET.BAT that has login commands. It also modifies your AUTOEXEC.BAT file to call the STARTNET.BAT file which runs the commands to connect to the network. The user is prompted to enter his or her password (if it is required).

The following commands may be in the STARTNET.BAT file.

    C:
    CD\NWCLIENT
    LSL.COM
    NE2000
    IPXODI
    VLM
    F:
    LOGIN username

These commands can also be entered in the AUTOEXEC.BAT instead of calling STARTNET.BAT or entered by the user.

NET.CFG

NET.CFG is the network configuration file. The workstation's connection software (LSL.COM, LAN driver, IPXODI, and VLM) reads commands from this file to configure the workstation environment. The following is a sample NET.CFG file:

Link Driver NE2000

    INT 3
    PORT 300
    MEM D0000
    FRAME Ethernet_802.2

NetWare DOS Requester

    FIRST NETWORK DRIVE = F

    Preferred Server = PCAGE

Supporting Windows Workstations

The NetWare client installation software is used to support MS Windows workstations on the network. This software copies specific files into Windows directories and modifies several Windows files. After the NetWare client software installation, the DOS Requester and Windows coordinate to provide server connection and login, network drive mappings, printer redirection, etc.

Installing Workstation Software

The NetWare client installation software is menu driven and installs both DOS and MS Windows workstations. This software copies the required files and modifies the appropriate configuration files.

To use the NetWare client installation software from the DOS prompt, do the following:

1. Insert the WSDOS_1 disk into a disk drive.
2. Change to the drive and type INSTALL.
3. Follow the instructions on the screen.

Review Questions

Q.1. Which one of the following is used to load VLMs into memory?

    a. VLM.EXE   b. DOS Requester

    c. NETx.EXE   d. LOAD.VLM

Q.2. Which is the right order to run workstation files?

    a. LSL, NE2000, IPXODI, VLM

    b. VLM, LSL, NE2000, IPXODI

    c. VLM, IPXODI, NE2000, LSL

    d. NE2000, VLM, LSL, IPXODI

Q.3. You must have the LASTDRIVE=Z command in _____ when using the DOS Requester.

    a. AUTOEXEC.BAT   b. CONFIG.SYS

    c. NET.CFG   d. STARTNET.BAT

Q.4. The workstation installation program creates a file called _____ in the NWCLIENT directory.

    a. CONFIG.SYS   b. STARTNET.BAT

c. AUTOEXEC.BAT   d. NET.CFG

Q.5. Which one of the following is the workstation network configuration file?

    a. CONFIG.SYS   b. AUTOEXEC.BAT
    c. NET.CFG   d. STARTUP.NCF

Q.6. What is wrong with the following NET.CFG file?

Link Driver NE2000
INT 3
PORT 300
MEM D0000
FRAME Ethernet_802.2

    a. INT should be IRQ   b. PORT should be I/O
    c. options are not indented   d. section heading is wrong

Chapter 9   Login Scripts

A login script contains commands that initialize environment variables and map network drives, etc. Like the DOS AUTOEXEC.BAT file, we put commands in login scripts that we want to execute automatically each time a user logs in. Login scripts are executed as part of the login procedure.

Types of Login Scripts

There are three different types of login scripts used by the file server.

1. System login script.
2. User login script.
3. Default login script.

Login scripts are executed in the order given above.

System Login Script

System login scripts contain commands for mapping network drives, mapping search drives, setting up environment variables, or setting commands that relate to all or a group(s) of users.

The system login script is created in SYSCON and saved in the SYS:PUBLIC directory as NET$LOG.DAT.

User Login Script

The user login script contains commands for individual users. This login script runs from the file called LOGIN in the user ID directory under the mail directory.

Default Login Script

If no user login script exists, a default login script will execute. The default login script is coded into the LOGIN.EXE file in the SYS:LOGIN. The default login script sets up the basic mappings for the system. This script cannot be edited.

If you do not want to execute the default login script for users who do not have user login scripts, use the NO_DEFAULT login script command in the system login script.

Login Script Commands

#

Use the number sign (#) to execute an external program (.EXE or .COM file) from within your login script. The login script will continue after the external program is exited.

Examples:

   #Capture nb ti=1 nff

Note: Do not run batch files using the # command. To run batch files or DOS internal command, use:

#command /c

Examples:

#command /c CLS (to execute the DOS CLS command)

#command /c Batch.bat (to execute the batch.bat file)

Do not run large programs using the # command. You may get error messages because the login script is held in memory when the # command is run. There may not be enough memory to run large programs.

ATTACH

Use ATTACH to connect to additional file servers. NetWare allows a user to attach to up to 8 file servers at the same time.

Note: No login scripts will be executed when you attach to a server. To execute login scripts, you use LOGIN command to login to the server. LOGIN command also logs you out from the previous server(s). ATTACH command allows you to connect to the multiple servers at the same time.

Example:

IF MEMBER OF "SALES" THEN BEGIN

ATTACH FS2

END

(The user will be prompted to enter variables not included with the ATTACH command, e.g., server name, user name, and password.)

BREAK ON/OFF

If you are using BREAK ON in your login script, you can press <Ctrl> C or <Ctrl><Break> to abort the execution of your login script. The default setting is BREAK OFF.

Note: BREAK ON is only used so you can abort the execution of the login script. Use DOS BREAK ON so you will be able to terminate the execution of any program by pressing <Ctrl><Break>.

COMSPEC

COMSPEC is used to specify the directory that DOS will use to reload the COMMAND.COM if it has been overwritten by an application. If you receive a message "Missing or invalid COMMAND.COM" after exiting from an application, use the COMSPEC command. COMSPEC should be set to reload COMMAND.COM from the network rather than from the local workstation drive.

Examples:

    MAP S3:= SYS:PUBLIC\MSDOS
    COMSPEC=S3:COMMAND.COM
       or
    COMSPEC=C:\DOS\COMMAND.COM

DISPLAY

This command is used to show the contents of a specified text file on your workstation screen during the login.

Example:

    DISPLAY SYS:PUBLIC\MESSAGES\MESSAGE1.TXT

DOS BREAK ON/OFF

Use DOS BREAK ON if you want to use <Ctrl><Break> to terminate the execution of a program.

DOS SET

Use SET to set a DOS environment variable.

Examples:

    DOS SET PSC = "PSPS1 P0"

        or

    SET PSC = "PSPS1 P0"

    SET username = "%LOGIN_NAME"

DOS VERIFY ON/OFF

Use DOS VERIFY ON if you want to verify that data copied to a local drive using the DOS COPY command can be read after copy. The NetWare copy command (NCOPY) verifies this automatically. Instead of using DOS VERIFY ON, you can use the DOS COPY command with /v option.

DRIVE

Use this to specify your default drive. This command will put the user in the specified drive.

Example:

    MAP J:=FS2/SYS:APPS/WORK
    DRIVE J:

The user will be in the WORK directory after logging in.

EXIT

EXIT is used to terminate the execution of the login script and to execute an external program (.EXE, .COM, or .BAT file). Any login script commands after the EXIT command will be ignored. If this command is used in the SYSTEM login script, then the USER login script or the DEFAULT login script will not be executed after the SYSTEM login script. The string that follows the EXIT command must be 14 characters or less including spaces.

Examples:

    EXIT

    or

    EXIT "NMENU MYMENU"

(Note that the string "NMENU MYMENU" is less than 14 characters.)

FDISPLAY

Use FDISPLAY to display a text file on your screen. FDISPLAY displays the specified text file in "filtered" format. It removes non-text characters (printing codes, etc.) so that only the text is displayed.

Example:

    FDISPLAY SYS:PUBLIC/MESSAGES/NOTE.TXT

FIRE PHASERS

This command makes the user's workstation produce sounds. This is mainly used to alert a user.

Examples:

    FIRE PHASER 3 TIMES
    or
    FIRE 3

GOTO

Use GOTO to execute a portion of the login script out of sequence. This command can be used to create loops (to repeat a sequence of commands).

Example:

    SET X="0"
    LOOP:
    SET X=<X>+"1"
    FIRE 3
    WRITE "Happy Happy Birthday!"
    IF <X> IS LESS THAN VALUE "10" THEN GOTO LOOP

The above statements will execute the FIRE 3 and WRITE commands 10 times. User will hear sound and see Birthday message 10 times.

IF...THEN...ELSE

Use IF...THEN...ELSE to execute commands if a certain condition logically exists. IF statements can be nested up to 10 levels.

Examples:

```
IF DAY_OF_WEEK ="Friday" THEN WRITE " Thank God it's Friday"

IF MEMBER OF "SUPER" THEN BEGIN
      MAP *1:=FS1/SYS:SYSTEM
      MAP S1:=FS1/SYS:SYSTEM
ELSE
      MAP *1:=FS1/SYS:USERS/%LOGIN_NAME
      MAP S1:=FS1/SYS:PUBLIC
END

IF MEMBER OF "WORDPERFECT" THEN BEGIN
      MAP G:=FS1/SYS:APPS/WP
ELSE
      IF MEMBER OF "WORD" THEN BEGIN
            MAP G:=FS1/SYS:APPS/WORD
      ELSE
            IF MEMBER OF "MultiMate" THEN BEGIN
                  MAP G:=FS1/SYS:APPS/MM
            END
      END
END
```

Note: See Novell Installation manual for the list of identifier variables that can be used with the IF command.

INCLUDE

Use INCLUDE if you want to run other login scripts (subscripts) from your current login script. Subscripts are text files that contain login script commands.

Example:

   INCLUDE SYS:PUBLIC/SUBSCRIP.TXT

MACHINE

MACHINE can be used to set the DOS machine name of the station to a specified name. The machine name can be up to 8 characters long. This command is necessary for some programs that run under PC DOS (such as NETBIOS).

Example:

   MACHINE="name"

MAP

The MAP command is the most important login script command. It maps a drive to a directory on the network.

Examples:

   MAP F:=SYS:PUBLIC
   MAP S1:=SYS:PUBLIC

NO_DEFAULT

If the NO_DEFAULT command is used in the system login script, then the default login script will not execute for users who do not have individual login scripts.

PAUSE

PAUSE or WAIT commands are used to create a pause in the execution of the login script. If you include PAUSE in the login script, the message "Strike a key when ready..." appears on the workstation screen. The login program waits for a key to be pressed before it executes the rest of the login script.

Examples:

>   PAUSE
>   or
>   WAIT

PCCOMPATIBLE

Use PCCOMPATIBLE when including a file name with the EXIT command on all IBM PC compatible workstations. If you have changed the long machine name of your IBM PC compatible computer to a different name (such as COMPAQ) to access the correct DOS version, you must use the PCCOMPATIBLE or COMPATIBLE command to inform the login program that your computer is an IBM PC compatible. Remember to use the PCCOMPATIBLE command before the EXIT command.

Example:

>   PCCOMPATIBLE

EXIT "FILER"

REMARK

Use REMARK, REM, an asterisk (*), or a semicolon (;) to insert any comments (explanatory text) into your login scripts. All texts starting with these symbols will be ignored.

Examples:

   REM This is a comment.

   REMARK This is also a comment.

   * Here we are starting search mappings.

   ; Here we are starting drive mappings.

SHIFT

Use SHIFT to shift the LOGIN command line parameters to the next variable. The command format is:
SHIFT [n]

where n is the number of places to shift, a positive number moves each % variable to the right and a negative number move each % variable to the left.

Like DOS batch files, you can use command line parameters with the LOGIN command. The parameter then can be used with the % sign according to their position. SHIFT is used to change (shift) this position.
For example, the following is the LOGIN command and its command line parameter values:

   LOGIN FS1/BOB WP WORD

%0=FS1
%1=BOB
%2=WP
%3=WORD

You can use the above values in your login script as follows:

IF "%2"="WP" THEN MAP S3:=FS1/SYS:APPS\WP

If you are using SHIFT in your login script, the values will be changed as follows:

%0=BOB
%1=WP
%2=WORD

Now you can use MAP.

IF "%2"="WORD" THEN MAP S3:=FS1/SYS:APPS\WORD

WRITE

Use WRITE to display messages when executing a login script. The format is:

WRITE "text"

Examples:

WRITE "Good "; greeting_time; ", BOB"
WRITE "Good %GREETING_TIME, BOB"

Note: Identifier variables enclosed in quotation marks must be preceded by percent sign (%) and typed in upper-case letters.

For more information about login scripts commands, see the NetWare 3.12 *Installation and Upgrade* manual.

Sample System and User Login Scripts

System Login Script

map display off
map ins s1:=fs1/sys:public
map ins s2:=fs1/sys:public/msdos
comspec=s2:command.com

* If you have different versions of DOS, do a mapping like this:
* map ins S2:=fs1/SYS:public/MSDOS/%OS_VERSION

IF MEMBER OF "SUPER" THEN BEGIN
    map *1:=fs1/sys:system

    Rem *1 represents first network drive
    Rem *2 represents second network drive and so on

    map ins s3:=fs1/sys:system

    map ins s4:=fs1/sys:apps/clipper5/lib

    map g:=fs1/sys:apps/wp52
END

map h:=fs1/sys:users/%login_name
map j:=fs1/sys:apps/work

write "Hello, %LOGIN_NAME Good %GREETING_TIME"

IF MEMBER OF "NETWORK_PRN" THEN BEGIN
    ; pound sign (#) executes a valid DOS or NetWare program

    #capture nb ti=1 nff
END

SET PSC = "PSps1 P0"

drive j:

User Login Script

if day = "09" and month_name = "May" then
    fire 4
    fire 5
    write "****** Happy Happy Birthday Bob! ******"
    fire 3
    fire 2
end

if day_of_week = "Monday" then
    exit "b_picm"
end
if day_of_week = "Tuesday" then
    exit "b_pictu"
end
if day_of_week = "Wednesday" then
    exit "b_picw"
end
if day_of_week = "Thursday" then
    exit "b_picth"
end
if day_of_week = "Friday" then
    exit "b_picfr"
end

Review Questions

Q.1. Login scripts are executed in which order?

    a. SYSTEM, USER   b. USER, SYSTEM

    c. DEFAULT, USER   d. DEFAULT, SYSTEM

Q.2. What is the name of the SYSTEM login script and where is it located?

    a. NET$LOG.DAT, PUBLIC

    b. NET$LOG.DAT, SYSTEM

    c. SYSLOGIN, PUBLIC

    d. LOGIN, SYSTEM

Q.3. A login script is executed each time a user _____ .

    a. boots the workstation   b. logs in to the system

    c. types LOGINSCRIPT   d. ATTACHes to a server

Q.4. Which of the following command lets you connect to the multiple servers at the same time?

    a. LOGIN   b. ATTACH

    c. CONNECT   d. SUPERVISOR

Chapter 9: Login Scripts

Q.5. You can connect to _____ server(s) at the same time.

    a. 1   b. 4

    c. 8   d. 16

Q.6. Which of the following commands lets you execute external programs from within your login scripts? (select all that are true)

    a. #   b. RUN

    c. CALL   d. EXIT

Q.7. The default login script is stored in the _____ .

    a. LOGIN.EXE, LOGIN directory

    b. LOGIN.EXE, PUBLIC directory

    c. NET$LOG.DAT, PUBLIC directory

    d. DEFAULT.DAT, PUBLIC directory

Q.8. To avoid execution of default login script you can do which of the following? (select all that are true)

    a. use EXIT command in SYSTEM login script

    b. use EXIT command in USER login script

    c. use NO_DEFAULT Command in SYSTEM login script

© 1993 - 95 · PC Age, Inc. All Rights Reserved · 20 Audrey Place · Fairfield, NJ 07004 · U.S.A. · Tel: 201-882-5370

d. use /ND option with LOGIN command

Q.9. To execute login script commands out of sequence, which of the following commands would you use?

    a. EXIT   b. GOTO
    c. ATTACH   d. LOOP

Q.10. Which of the following login script commands is related to COMMAND.COM?

    a. COMSPEC   b. DOS SET
    c. COMMAND   d. DOS BREAK

Q.11. To execute a login script from within a login script which of the following commands would you use?

    a. CALL   b. EXIT
    c. #   d. INCLUDE

Subscript

Q.12. IF statements can be nested up to _____ levels.

    a. 8   b. 16
    c. 4   d. 10

Q.13. Which of the following characters cannot be used to start a comment in a login script?

    a. #   b. ;

    c. *   d. REM

Q.14. Which of the following commands is not correct?

    a. WRITE "Good"; greeting_time; ", BOB"

    b. WRITE " Good %GREETING_TIME, BOB"

    c. EXIT "NMENU MYMENU.DAT"

    d. # NMENU MYMENU.DAT

Q.15. You cannot modify the SYSTEM login script by using which of the following?

    a. SYSCON "Supervisor Options"

    b. EDIT.NLM

    c. Any text editor

    d. FILER

Q.16. To make sure the user is in his home (default) directory when he/she logs in, which of the following commands would you use?

    a. DRIVE H: b. DEFAULT H:

    c. GOTO H: d. DIR H:

Q.17. If you are not sure about the first network drive letter, which of the following would you use to set up drive mapping?

    a. F: b. *1

    c. FIRST   d. NEXT

Chapter 10   NetWare Menus

Overview

In the user friendly computer world, the availability of menus is a basic feature. NetWare has offered this service from early releases, and supplies a more sophisticated process NMENU with 3.12. This not only offers greater facility but also requires less memory than earlier processes.

NMENU, like other menu processes, displays a list of preset operations that may be selected by the user without concern for exact entry of commands and options. Any necessary additional information will be prompted with the display of a suitable default.

Preparing a Menu

To create a menu, we create a menu script file using the defined commands. This file can be created by using any DOS text (ASCII) editor. This file should have extension .SRC (source). This file is then compiled with MENUMAKE program that creates a .DAT file. Then you can run your menu with the NMENU program.

A Simple Sample Menu

```
Application Menu
A. WordPerfect
B. Database
C. DOS Prompt
D. Logout
```

Figure 10-1

```
MENU 01, Application Menu
   ITEM WordPerfect
      EXEC WP
   ITEM Database
      EXEC dbase
   ITEM DOS Prompt
      EXEC DOS
   ITEM Logout
      EXEC LOGOUT
```

Source Commands

There are two categories of source commands: organizational, and control. The organizational commands define the structure of the menu (what menu will look like on the screen) and the control commands perform an action, such as running an application or prompting the user for input.

Organizational Commands

There are two organizational commands MENU and ITEM. The MENU command establishes the main menu or sub-menus and ITEM defines the options (selections) of each menu component.

1. MENU number,menu_name

a. number

Each menu section must be given a unique number from 1 to 255. This is used for correct reference of sub-menus. The first menu in the file is considered the main menu but must also have a number.

b. menu_name

This is the title to be displayed in the menu. It may be up to 40 characters long including embedded spaces.

Example:

    MENU 1,Main Menu

    MENU 5,Directory/File Stuff

2. ITEM item_name {options}

a. item_name

The item name will be displayed as a menu selection. It may be up to 40 characters with imbedded spaces like the menu_name. Choices will be displayed with a prefixed letter of the alphabet in the order of their entry.

If a certain letter is desired, then it may be selected by using the ^(caret) as a prefix to that letter.

    Example: ITEM ^XLogout

b. {options}

There are four options that may be selected to affect the execution of the ITEM. They are entered within a single set of braces {}.

- BATCH   This will allow 32K of memory to be released during the execution of the item by removing the menu program from memory. It is recommended for application selections to avoid memory conflicts. It should not be used when the actions are standard DOS/NetWare commands or utilities.

- CHDIR   This option will restore the original default directory at the end of the action items. It is automatically invoked with the BATCH option and is recommended for any action that might change directories.

- PAUSE   This operates in the same fashion as the DOS batch file PAUSE and displays a message " Press any key to continue".

- SHOW   This option will display the DOS and NetWare commands invoked to show the action. Commands such as COPY or DIR will be shown in the upper-left corner of the screen.

Example:

ITEM Word_Perfect {BATCH}

Control Commands

There are six commands in the control category: EXEC, SHOW, LOAD, GETO, GETR, and GETP.

1. EXEC command

The command being executed is usually a DOS or NetWare command. EXEC is also used to run applications or to select standard utilities. There are also four special EXEC forms.

   a. EXEC EXIT: This will terminate the NMENU process and return the user to the standard prompt. Users cannot exit from the menu unless this command is included in the menu. Type EXIT in uppercase; otherwise it will not work.

   b. EXEC DOS: This will temporarily take the user to the operating system prompt. When the user has completed any desired actions, the command EXIT will return control to NMENU. Type DOS in uppercase; otherwise it will not work.

   c. EXEC LOGOUT: This will terminate the NMENU operation and logout the user from the Network.

   d. EXEC CALL: This is the recommended form to invoke DOS batch files.

2. SHOW number

This is how sub-menus are invoked under NMENU. The number is the one assigned to the sub-menu to be displayed. These sub-menus are in the same file with main menu.

Examples:

```
          MENU 1, Filing
            ITEM NetWare
             SHOW 10
            ITEM DOS style
             SHOW 20
```

```
        MENU 10, Net Services
         ITEM Create
          EXEC FILER
         ITEM Restrict Use
          EXEC DSPACE
        MENU 20, DOS Diddling Does
         ITEM Where Am I?
          EXEC DIR
         ITEM Start a file {SHOW}
          EXEC COPY CON
```

3. LOAD file_name

From within NMENU you may also invoke other compiled menus (.DAT files) by using the LOAD command.

Example:

```
        MENU 10,Bob's Menu Choices
         ITEM Bob's Favorites
          LOAD BOB1
         ITEM Bob's less favorites
          LOAD BOB1
         ITEM Bob's unfavorites
          LOAD BOB10
```

Getting User Input

The other three commands (GETO, GETR, GETP) prompt for user input. The format is:

   GETx prompt {prepend}length,prefill, {append} where x represents O, R, or P.

a. prompt

The prompt is what will be displayed to the user in requesting the input.

b. {prepend}

This is a fixed value added to the user input. It is often a simple space indicated by { }.

c. Length

This is the maximum number of characters allowed in the user input field.

d. Prefill

This will default to spaces for the user input. It may also be used to enter a specific default that will be displayed in the prompt window.

e. {append}

This is an optional addition to follow the user input.

The options for GETx are:

4. GETO

This allows for entering an input or taking a default.

Example:

> GETO Which files you want to see ? { }20,*.* /P, {}
> EXEC NDIR
>
> Here a user can enter either files specification or Press F10 to select the default (*.* /p).

5. GETR

This requires user input. If none is entered the action will not take place and the user must return to the menu selection phase.

Example:

    GETR Enter program name to run:{}30,,{}
    EXEC

6. GETP

This allows the input from the user to be tagged for further use. The tags are %1,%2, and so on. When you use GETP, the user input can be used by more than one EXEC command. The P in GETP stands for Parameters.

Example:

    GETP Source file?:{}11,,{}
    GETP Destination File?:{}11,,{}
    EXEC NCOPY %1 %2
    EXEC DIR %2

The GETx's commands must be entered between the ITEM line and the EXEC line associated with it. A maximum of 100 GET commands are allowed per ITEM. The end of user input is indicated with <F10> rather than <ENTER>.

Compiling Menus

Once a menu has been prepared in a file, it must then be compiled by the program MENUMAKE. This program assumes the file will have the extension .SRC . It will process the information and enter the results in a file with the same name but with the extension .DAT in the same directory as the .SRC file. Any source commands that violate the NMENU requirements will be noted by error messages. The process may be repeated on edited files and the existing .DAT will be overwritten. The command format for the MENUMAKE command is:

    MENUMAKE [path]file_name

Executing Menus

Once a menu has been successfully compiled the .DAT file may then be executed by NMENU.

    NMENU [path]file_name

It is recommended that a directory be established to hold the executable menus available to all users. This would have suitable trustee rights for the group EVERYONE similar to PUBLIC. Likewise each user might have a similar directory assigned in their area for specialized menus created for them.

Compatibility with Earlier Versions

In 2.x and 3.11 the menu service was performed by MENU that acted as an interpreter of ASCII text files. In order to provide compatibility with these old menus, 3.12 includes a program to perform a conversion from the earlier form to one suitable for NMENU.

The earlier MENU dealt with ASCII text files with extension .MNU. The program MENUCNVT will use such a file to create a file with the extension .SRC suitable for compilation by MENUMAKE. This will take place in the same directory and leaves the .MNU untouched. The command format for MENUCNVT is:

    MENUCNVT [path]file_name

After the file has been converted it is recommended that the .SRC file be examined to see that a reasonable translation has taken place. This would be especially important for menus with tagged options, several sub-menus, or user input.

Once the conversion has been accepted, the .SRC may be compiled by MENUMAKE to provide a similar menu in the new system.

Practice Example:

```
        MENU 01, Main Menu
          ITEM Applications
            SHOW 05
          ITEM NetWare Utilities
            SHOW 10
          ITEM DOS Prompt
            EXEC DOS
          ITEM LOGOUT
            EXEC LOGOUT

        MENU 05, Applications
          ITEM WordPerfect {CHDIR}
            EXEC CD \APPS\WP
            EXEC WP

          ITEM DATABASE
            EXEC dbase

        MENU 10, NetWare Utilities
          ITEM ^1Menu Utilities
            SHOW 12
          ITEM ^2Command Line Utilities
            SHOW 14

        MENU 12, Menu Utilities
          ITEM SYSCON   {BATCH}
            EXEC syscon
          ITEM  FILER   {BATCH}
            EXEC filer
          ITEM SESSION  {BATCH}
            EXEC session
          ITEM PCONSOLE {BATCH}
            EXEC pconsole

        MENU 14, Command Line Utilities
          ITEM Directory Listing   {SHOW PAUSE}
            GETO Enter File Name or Path:{ }20,*.*,{ }
            EXEC NDIR

          ITEM Copy Files  {SHOW PAUSE}
            GETP Enter Source Name { }20,,{ }
            GETP Enter Destination Name { }20,,{ }
            EXEC NCOPY %1 %2
            EXEC DIR %2

          ITEM Run Any Program {BATCH SHOW CHDIR}
            GETR Enter Program Name:{ }30,,{ }
            EXEC
```

Review Questions

Q.1. The proper steps to use a NetWare menu are:

1. Create a menu script file
2. Compile using MENUMAKE
3. Run using NMENU

a. 1, 2, 3   b. 2, 3, 1
c. 3, 2, 1   d. 1, 3, 2

Q.2. The extension for a menu script file and the compiled file are _____ ?

a. .DAT and .SRC   b. .SRC and .DAT
c. .SRC and USR   d. .SRC and MNU

Q.3. A menu is created so that _____ . (select the one that is not true)

a. users can run applications without knowing the exact commands
b. Users do not have to remember locations of applications
c. Users can enjoy a simpler working environment
d. Users can run applications without having rights in applications directories

Q.4. Which of the following are Organizational commands?

    a. MENU   b. NMENU
    c. ITEM   d. OPTIONS

Q.5. Which one of the following is not a Control command?

    a. EXEC   b. LOAD
    c. MENU   d. GETO

Q.6. Which of the following commands would you not use for user input?

    a. GETx   b. GETO
    c. GETR   d. GETP

Q.7. To allow a user to see a directory, which one of the following commands would you use?

    a. GETx   b. GETO
    c. GETR   d. GETP

Q.8. To allow a user to run an application, which one of the following commands would you use?

    a. GETx   b. GETO

    c. GETR   d. GETP

Q.9. To allow a user to copy a file, which one of the following commands would you use?

    a. GETx   b. GETO

    c. GETR   d. GETP

Chapter 11   Installing Applications

Installing Applications on a Network

Here are some points you should consider before you install any application on the network.

- Before you purchase any application, make sure it is compatible with NetWare 3.12. Contact the software vendor or reseller. Compatibility information is also available on NetWire and on Novell's Electronic Bulletin Board.

- If more than one user will be using the application at the same time, make sure the application is multi-user.

- Create a directory to install the application. Some applications automatically create the directory. Follow the application's documentation to install the application.

- Flag the application files as needed.

- Users must be given appropriate trustee rights to the directory to use the application. Usually R F rights are sufficient.

- You may have to set up the workstation environment by modifying the CONFIG.SYS file.

Review Questions

Q.1. When buying an application for the network, what would you not do? (select all that are true)

    a. make sure the application is NetWare compatible.

    b. make sure the application is multi-user, if more then one user will be using it at the same time

    c. make sure the application supports word processing

    d. make sure the application can be installed from the server

Q.2. Which one of the following steps does not sound right when installing an application on the network?

    a. make sure the application is network (NetWare) compatible

    b. make sure the application is multi-user

    c. install the application from the server

    d. Flag the application files as needed

Q.3. Which one of the following steps does not sound right to install an application on the network?

    a. install the user application from the workstation

    b. Flag the application files as needed

c. give users appropriate rights

d. change server's CONFIG.SYS

Chapter 12   Backup

Overview

Storage Management Services (SMS) refers to NetWare services designed to back up and restore data. The SMS modules support backup and restore activities independent of the hardware and file system (DOS, OS2, MAC, NFS, etc.). The system manager or supervisor should take responsibility to see that backup is done for the network files as well as for any significant hard disks at the workstations. Without this management step serious problems could result from a disk failure.

Strategies for Backup and Restore

The ultimate backup service would be to save every file when it is created or modified. This would be costly in both time and materials and so there are three forms of backup:

- Full
- Incremental
- Differential

The first form is a full backup that saves all data on a periodic basis. This should always be done. Depending on the activity of the system, this could be measured in weeks or months. NetWare and other operating systems supply a file attribute indicating whether a file is new or modified. This is often called the archive bit and is used by backup programs as a possible selection criteria. The backup process then may clear or leave this attribute bit set. Full backups normally clear (set it to 0; all new or modified files have archive bit set to 1) the archive bit. One of the other two forms is selected to be used with the full backup. Since they have different selection methods only one should be chosen between full backups.

Incremental Backup

This form will select only the new or modified files as determined by the archive bit. After saving the file, the bit is cleared. This method is faster to back up because it backs up only files modified or created after the full backup or after the last incremental backup.

Differential Backup

This form also selects only the new or modified files by the archive bit but does not clear it after saving the file. This method takes more time to back up because it backs up all new or modified files since the last full backup (not just since the last differential backup).

Restore Strategies

If it is necessary to restore the system data from backup, then the last full backup will be used first. Then, depending on whether you have employed the incremental or differential strategy, one or more additional backups will be required.

If the incremental form was used, then each incremental backup must be used in their proper order. If the differential backup form was used then only the last of these backups is needed. The trade off between the forms is that the incremental method is simpler in performing the backup since only the new or modified files since the last incremental backup will be saved. But upon restoring, greater effort is required. The differential form requires greater effort at each backup, since all new or modified files since the last full backup will be selected. The advantage is that to restore the system data, all new or modified files will be in a single location.

The two strategies could be tested but only one should be used between full backups.

Backup Responsibilities

The person performing the backups needs Read and File Scan rights to the files and passwords of the systems involved in the backup (host servers, target servers, workstations, etc.).

Novell Supplied Services

Novell supplies SBACKUP for SMS. This is designed to run on a file server with access primarily to file server files. There are options available to extend this service to hard disks at DOS or OS/2 workstations. The file server to perform this task should have a suitable backup device, usually a tape drive and should provide the service for any other file server on the network. Following terms are used for SBACKUP procedures:

SBACKUP Process

The file server with the backup device is termed the host and uses the SBACKUP.NLM for this. The file server to receive the service of backup is termed the target and requires the TSA312.NLM. The Target Service Agent (TSA) is also available for 3.11 file servers as TSA311.NLM. The TSAs require other support NLMs like CLIB that may already be loaded.

1. The target is established first. At the target file server, which may also be the host, TSA312.NLM is loaded along with other support NLMs.

2. Next the host server has SBACKUP loaded. This routine then has a series of menus. A log of any backup is retained on the host to direct any later restore activity.

3. Since there are several compatible backup devices, if more than one is available at the host, one will be chosen. The driver for the device is then loaded.

4. The target is selected from servers with TSA enabled.

    Note: At this point the backup or restore procedure is chosen. The following assumes backup.

5. The data and type of backup is selected: full, incremental, or differential.

6. The backup is performed.

7. The target of the backup may then be cleared of its TSA and specific support programs.

8. Another target may then be selected and the process repeats from step 4. When the backup or restore procedure is completed the host may be cleared of SBACKUP and its device driver. SBACKUP should be unloaded first to ensure that all connections with the driver are properly cleared. A serious error may occur otherwise.

Review Questions

Q.1. Which of the following backup methods takes less time but requires more disks?

    a. Full   b. incremental

    c. differential   d. SBACKUP

Q.2. Which of the following backup methods does not clear (set it to zero) the archive bit of the files?

    a. Full   b. incremental

    c. differential   d. SBACKUP

Q.3. Which of the following backup methods is easier when performing a backup but more difficult when restoring?

    a. Full   b. incremental

    c. differential   d. SBACKUP

Q.4. SBACKUP can be used to backup workstation's disks?

   a. true
   b. false
   c. only for DOS and OS/2 workstations
   d. only for DOS and MAC workstations

PCONSOLE

PCONSOLE is the main utility to manage printing. We use PCONSOLE to setup print queues, print servers, and printers.

Network Printing Steps

- Creating queues.
- Creating print server account.
- Defining printers.
- Assigning queues to printers.
- Loading print server program.
- Running RPRINTER (if using remote printer).

Creating Queues

A print queue is actually a subdirectory of the SYS:SYSTEM directory. It holds the print jobs until the print server sends them to the printer. A queue directory is created using a queue ID number and has the extension QDR. To create a queue, do the following:

1. Run the PCONSOLE command from any prompt.
2. Select "Print Queue Information".
3. Press <Ins> to create a new queue and type the queue name, e.g., Q1.
4. Press <Esc> to go back to the "Available Options" menu.

Creating a Print Server Account and Defining Printers

1. Select "Print Server Information".
2. Press <Ins> to create a new print server and type the name, e.g., PS1.

Chapter 13: Printing

3. Press <Enter> to select PS1.
4. Select "Print Server Configuration".
5. Select "Printer Configuration".
6. Select printer number and then complete the "Printer Configuration" form.
7. Change the name of the printer if you like.
8. Highlight the type of printer from the list and press <Enter>.
    You will select Parallel, LPT or Serial, COM, if attaching printers directly to the file server.

    Select Remote Parallel, LPT or Remote Serial, COM, if attaching printers to a workstation.
9. Use interrupts: Yes or No. Usually we will select yes here. If you do not know the interrupt or have an interrupt conflict, then you can select "No" here. If you select "No", polled mode will be used for printing.
10. Press <Esc> to save changes and exit.

Assigning Print Queues to Printers

1. Go to the "Print Server Configuration Menu".
2. Select "Queues Serviced by Printer".
3. Select printer.
4. Press <Ins> to select a queue.
5. Accept priority 1 or change if you like (1 is highest and 10 is lowest).
6. Press <Esc> until you exit from PCONSOLE.

© 1993 - 95 · PC Age, Inc. All Rights Reserved · 20 Audrey Place · Fairfield, NJ 07004 · U.S.A. · Tel: 201-882-5370

Loading the Print Server Program

Decide which print server program (PSERVER.NLM, PSERVER.EXE or PSERVER.VAP) you want to use and load the program for the appropriate computer (3.12 file server, dedicated workstation, or 286 file server, respectively).

Loading PSERVER.NLM on the File Server

If you want to use 3.12 file server as print server computer, type the following at the console prompt:

: Load PSERVER PS1

(where PS1 is print server name)

You can put the load server command in the AUTOEXEC.NCF file.

Note: You can down the print server in two ways:

- Using the UNLOAD command like:

    :UNLOAD PSERVER PS1

- Selecting the DOWN option under Server Info in PCONSOLE.

Loading PSERVER.EXE on Dedicated Workstation

To use a dedicated workstation as a print server, do the following at the DOS workstation:

1. Place the following command in the NET.CFG file:

    SPX connections=60

2. Login to the network from the workstation you want to use as a dedicated Print Server.

3. Run PSERVER, like

    PSERVER PS1

You can put the PSERVER command in the AUTOEXEC.BAT file. PSERVER.EXE requires the loading of some additional files. For a list of these files, see the *Print Server* manual. You can either copy these files to your local drive (so PSERVER.EXE can load them) or first log in and then load them from the PUBLIC directory.

Note: A dedicated workstation print server can be brought down only by selecting the DOWN option under Server Info in PCONSOLE.

Running RPRINTER

To use a printer attached directly to your workstation as a remote network printer, at the workstation prompt, type

   RPRINTER Printserver printnumber <Enter>

(RPRINTER.EXE and other related files are in the SYS:PUBLIC directory).

If you have any interrupt conflicts (slow or sporadic printing are indications of interrupt conflicts), you can use the polled mode by using the -P option with the RPRINTER command:

    RPRINTER printserver print number -P

Polled mode printing (not using an interrupt) is slower than interrupt mode (using an interrupt) printing.

You can put RPRINTER command in AUTOEXEC.BAT file.

RPRINTER.EXE requires the loading of some additional files. For a list of these files, see the *Print Server* manual. You can either copy these files to your local drive (RPRINTER.EXE can load them) or first log in and then load them from the PUBLIC directory.

Chapter 13: Printing

```
NetWare Print Console V1.51    Monday September 17, 1993    6 : 43 pm
                    User SUPERVISOR On File Server BILL
```

```
           Available Options
        Change Current File Server
        ⇒ Print Queue Information
        ⇒ Print Server Information
```

```
      Print Queues
        Laser
        Pana
```

```
      Print Queue Information
        Current Print Job Entries
        Current Queue Status
        Currently Attached Servers
        Print Queue ID
        Queue Operators
        Queue Servers
        Queue Users
```

```
      Print Servers
        PS1
        PS2
```

```
      Print Server Information
        Changes Password
        Full Name
        ⇒ Print Server Configuration
        Print Server ID
        Print Server Operators
        Print Server Users
```

```
      Print Server Configuration Menu
        File Servers To Be Serviced
        Notify List for Printer
        Printer Configuration
        Queues Serviced by Printer
```

Figure 13-1(a) The PCONSOLE Utility.

```
┌─────────────────────────────────────────────────────────┐
│  NetWare Print Console V1.51   Monday September 17, 1993   6 : 43 pm │
│           User  SUPERVISOR On File Server BILL          │
└─────────────────────────────────────────────────────────┘
```

Configured Printers	
Panasonic	0
HPIIIp	1
Not Installed	2
Not Installed	3
Not Installed	4
Not Installed	5

Print Server Configuration Menu
File Servers To Be Serviced
Notify List for Printer
Printer Configuration
⇒Queues Serviced by Printer

Defined Printers	
Panasonic	0
HPIIIp	1

File Server	Queue	Priority
PCAGE	PANA	1
PCAGE	LASER	2

Figure 13-1(b) The PCONSOLE Utility.

Chapter 13: Printing

The CAPTURE Command

The CAPTURE command redirects output originally destined for a workstation's LPT ports to network printers, queues, or files. Use CAPTURE to print from applications that are not network compatible, to print screen dumps, and to save data to a network file.

The command format for CAPTURE is:

CAPTURE [options...]

CAPTURE Options

SHow	Form=form or n
NOTIfy	Copies=n
NoNOTIfy	Tabs=n
TImeout=n TI	NoTabs
Autoendcap	NoBanner NB
NoAutoendcap	NAMe=name
Local=n	Banner=bannername
Server=fileserver	FormFeed FF
Queue=queuename	NoFormFeed NNF
CReate=path	Keep
Job=jobconfiguration	

The above options are available with the CAPTURE command. We can use the abbreviated form of the options in the command format. We can set up an unchanging print configuration in the

© 1993 - 95 · PC Age, Inc. All Rights Reserved · 20 Audrey Place · Fairfield, NJ 07004 · U.S.A. · Tel: 201-882-5370

13-11

PRINTCON utility. If we do not specify any options data is printed according to the default configuration in PRINTCON.

Example: CAPTURE Q=EPSON NB NFF TI=1

We can also put the CAPTURE command in the system login script or the user script.

Ending the CAPTURE Command

We must end CAPTURE to send our data to a network printer to be printed or to a file to be saved. We can end CAPTURE in one of the following ways:

   Using the Autoendcap Option.

   Using the TImeout Option.

   Using the ENDCAP Command.

AUTOENDCAP sends data to the printer when we exit an application. AUTOENDCAP saves several different screens or files from the same application to the same network file.

TIMEOUT is useful if we want to print something from an application without exiting the application.

The ENDCAP command sends data to the printer and ends the CAPTURE of an LPT port. Users may want to use ENDCAP to print to a locally attached printer.

The following options can be used with the ENDCAP command:

ALL

This option ends the capture of all LPT ports.

CAncel

This option is used to end the capture of LPT1. This also discards any data without printing it.

CancelALL

This option is used to end the capture of all LPT: ports. It also discards any data without printing it.

CancelLocal=n

This option is used to end the capture of the specified LPT: port and to discard any data without printing it. n can be 1, 2 or 3.

Local=n

This option is used to end the capture of the specified LPT: port. n can be 1, 2, or 3.

Network Printing from MS Windows

You can send print jobs to network printers from Windows by using the NetWare User Tools for Windows. The NetWare Users Tools for Windows allows you to use the CAPTURE command, the ENDCAP command, to make a capture permanent for Windows, etc. Changes made with NetWare User Tools are the same as changes made using the CAPTURE command from outside of Windows, that is, they modify the DOS Requester environment and remain in effect even if you exit MS Windows.

The NPRINT Command

Like the DOS PRINT command, NPRINT allows users to print files from outside an application to a network printer. Most NPRINT options are the same as for CAPTURE. These options can be specified in the NPRINT command or can be set in PRINTCON.

The command format for the NPRINT command is

>   NPRINT path [option...]

NPRINT Options

NOTIfy	Tabs=n	NoNOTIfy
NoTabs	PrintServer=printserver	NoBanner
Server=fileserver	NAMe=name	Queue=queuename
Banner=bannername	Job=jobconfiguration	NoFormFeed
Form=form or n	FormFeed	Copies=n
Delete		

These are the 16 options available with the NPRINT command. We can use the abbreviated form of the options in the command format.

Example:

NPRINT AUTOEXEC.BAT Q=Laser NB NFF

SPOOL (Console Command)

To set up a default print queue for NPRINT and CAPTURE, use the SPOOL command at the file server:

   :SPOOL 0 Queue_Name   (e.g., Q0)

SPOOL can also be used to redirect print jobs sent to a printer number. Most network applications send print jobs to a print queue. However, some old applications (that are compatible with the old version of NetWare) send print jobs to network printers instead of queues. For these applications, the SPOOL console command can be used to redirect the job to the queue. Use SPOOL as follows:

   :SPOOL printer# [to] Queuename

Replace printer# with the SPOOL number (0 through 4)

Example:

   :SPOOL 1 to Q_EPSON

Note: To save the spooler assignments permanently, include them in the system AUTOEXEC.NCF file.

PRINTDEF *Printer Define   37*

PRINTDEF is used to customize individual printers. We can use PRINTDEF to set up a database of printer definitions and to define forms. A user can have up to 37 different printer definitions stored.

PRINTCON → *Printer Config*

PRINTCON is used to customize print jobs. We use **PRINTCON** to define preferred print options and to set them up as standard configurations. PRINTCON serves as a database for printing with CAPTURE, NPRINT, and PCONSOLE. In PRINTCON we use the printer definitions created in PRINTDEF to set up complete configurations for specific print jobs.

RCONSOLE - How These on Floppy
To use Rconsole from remotely manage server

- *A console.exe*
- *R console.exe*
- *SYS$MSG.DAT*
- *$RUN.OVL*
- *Rconsole Help*
- *SYS$ERR.DAT*
- ~~Modem.CFG~~
- ~~Phone.nr~~

Network Printing Users

Table 13-1 shows printing tasks that can be accomplished by different categories of users. The Supervisor or equivalent has control over all printing functions.

Task	S	PQO	PQU	PSO	PSU
Create or delete print queues	X				
Modify print queues	X	X			
Use print queues	X		X		
Manipulate others' print queue entries	X	X			
Manipulate own print queue entries	X		X		
Create or delete print servers and printers	X				
Modify print servers or printers	X			X	
Monitor the print server	X				X

S	Supervisor or equivalent
PQO	Print Queue Operator
PQU	Print Queue User
PSO	Print Server Operator
PSU	Print Server User

Table 13-1

Note that print queue or print server operators cannot create or delete queues or print servers, they can only manage them. Only supervisor or equivalent can create or delete queues and print servers.

When print queues are created, the group Everyone is made a print queue user, and Supervisor is made a print queue and print server operator. Supervisor equivalent is not automatically made a print queue or print server operator, but he can make himself print queue or print server operator. Use PCONSOLE to assign a special operator or to restrict the users.

Review Questions

Q.1. For a dedicated print server which of the following would you run at the workstation.

    a. PSERVER.NLM   b. PSERVER.EXE
    c. PSERVER.VAP   d. RPRINTER.EXE

Q.2. Print jobs are stored on the server in subdirectories under _____ .

    a. SYS:SYSTEM   b. SYS:QUEUE
    c. SYS:SYSTEM\QUEUE   d. SYS:PSERVER

Q.3. When using a workstation as a dedicated print server, print jobs are stored in _____ .

    a. directories on the dedicated workstation
    b. directories on the file server
    c. QUEUE directory on the file server
    d. PSERVER directory on the workstation

Q.4. Printing services are provided by the NetWare operating system.

    a. true

    b. false

    c. only when using file server as a print server

    d. only when using a dedicated print server

Q.5. What must you do before you define a printer?

    a. create queue

    b. create print server account

    c. load print server

    d. run RPRINTER

Q.6. What must you do before you run RPRINTER? (select the one that is not true)

    a. define a remote printer

    b. assign a queue to the remote printer

    c. run PSERVER.EXE

    d. load Print Server

Chapter 13: Printing

Q.7. You must use SPX CONNECTIONS=60 in the NET.CFG file before you run _____ ?

    a. RPRINTER.EXE   b. PSERVER.EXE
    c. PSERVER.NLM   d. PCONSOLE

Q.8. Which of the following commands must be used before you can print on a network printer?

    a. PCONSOLE   b. CAPTURE
    c. PSERVER.EXE   d. RPRINTER
    e. You can print on a network without using any of these commands

Q.9. Which one of the following capture commands is not correct?

    a. CAPTURE Q=EPSON NB NFF TI=1
    b. CAPTURE QUEUE= EPSON
    c. CAPTURE NB NFF TI=1
    d. CAPTURE QUEUE=EPSON PORT=1 NB NFF

Q.10. Which of the following cannot be used to END the CAPTURE of a print job?

    a. Autoendcap option
    b. Timeout option
    c. ENDCAP command
    d. ENDCAP option in PCONSOLE

Q.11. To print from within an application right away, you would use _____ .

    a. Autoendcap option
    b. Timeout option
    c. ENDCAP command
    d. ENDCAP option in PCONSOLE

Q.12. To print from an application when you exit the application, you would use the _____ .

    a. Autoendcap option
    b. Timeout option
    c. ENDCAP command
    d. ENDCAP option in PCONSOLE

Q.13. To print outputs from multiple applications at your convenience, you would use the _____ .

    a. NoAutoendcap option with CAPTURE and ENDCAP command
    b. Timeout option with CAPTURE and ENDCAP command

c. Autoendcap option with CAPTURE and ENDCAP command

d. ENDCAP command

Q.14. To print to a network printer you use _____ . To print to a local printer you use _____ .

    a. CAPTURE, ENDCAP   b. ENDCAP, CAPTURE

    c. CAPTURE, RPRINTER   d. RPRINTER, PSERVER

Q.15. Which one of the following is not used to send print jobs to a queue?

    a. PCONSOLE   b. CAPTURE

    c. NPRINT   d. RPRINTER

Q.16. To delete a printer so that users cannot print, you would use _____ .

    a. PCONSOLE   b. PRINTDEF

    c. PRINTCON   d. CAPTURE

Q.17. To define a printer for network printing, you must use
_____ . (select all that are true)

    a. PCONSOLE   b. PRINTDEF

    c. PRINTCON   d. CAPTURE

Q.18. To control printers for different types of printing (bold, different font sizes, etc.) which of the following utilities is used?

    a. PCONSOLE   b. PRINTDEF

    c. PRINTCON   d. CAPTURE

Q.19. To start, stop, or rewind printers which of the following utilities is used?

    a. PCONSOLE   b. PRINTDEF

    c. PRINTCON   d. CAPTURE

Q.20. To create a database of different printing options, which of the following utilities is used?

    a. PCONSOLE   b. PRINTDEF

    c. PRINTCON   d. CAPTURE

Chapter 14   Remote Management

Remote management allows us to manage all of our NetWare file servers (3.1 and above) from one location. After setting up a remote console at a workstation, we can control all the file servers that have the appropriate software loaded. We have greater control of file server security when we use remote management. Remote management works with the NetWare 3.1x operating system. Remote management is provided by **Remote Management Facility (RMF)** software bundled with NetWare 3.12. We can perform the following functions with remote management:

- We can use console commands as we would at the file server console.

- We can scan directories and edit text files in both DOS and NetWare partitions on a remote file server.

- We can transfer files to (but not from) a remote file server.

- We can add an existing NetWare 3.1x file server to an established remote management network.

- We can reboot a file server from a remote console.

© 1993 - 95 · PC Age, Inc. All Rights Reserved · 20 Audrey Place · Fairfield, NJ 07004 · U.S.A. · Tel: 201-882-5370

Only **Supervisor** and **Remote Console Operators** can use remote management. These users must have appropriate rights and must pass password security checks before they can access a file server from a remote console. If the MONITOR keyboard lock is set, the password must be entered to gain access.

Remote Console Operator

Basically any user who has the rights R and F in the SYS:SYSTEM directory can work as a Remote Console Operator.

NetWare Supervisor

A Supervisor can open a remote console session using either the remote or the Supervisor password. However, the volume SYS must be mounted in order for the Supervisor password to work. A NetWare Supervisor cannot create users or assign rights from a remote console.

Using Remote Management

The software that manages the remote console does not disable the regular console keyboard. Remote management supports concurrent connections to a file server. It is also helpful for troubleshooting and for training purposes. The remote console can initiate a server process and then can terminate the session without affecting the process.

File Server Software for Remote Management

Both file server and workstation software are needed for remote management. Files with an .NLM extension are loaded from the file server.

REMOTE.NLM

This loadable module manages the reception and transmission of keyboard and monitor information to and from the communication drivers.

RSPX.NLM

This loadable module is a communication driver that provides SPX support for REMOTE.NLM.

RS232.NLM

This loadable module is an asynchronous communication driver that initiates the file server's communication port and transfers screen and keystroke information to and from REMOTE.NLM.

Workstation Software for Remote Management

Note: Files with an .EXE extension are loaded from the workstation.

ACONSOLE.EXE

This utility works like many standard communication programs in that it allows control of a workstation modem (to dial, hang up, and so forth). This utility also controls the transfer of screen and keystroke information to and from the remote file server.

RCONSOLE.EXE

This utility is a communication program that turns a workstation into a remote console. This utility also controls the transfer of screen and keystroke information to and from the remote file server.

Note: To prevent unauthorized access to file servers, keep remote management software, particularly RCONSOLE.EXE in the SYSTEM directory.

Communication Link Types

Three types of connections can be established with file servers on local and wide area networks. These are **Direct Link**, **Asynchronous Link**, and **Redundant Link**.

Direct Link

In the Direct Link method, a remote session with a file server is established from a workstation. The workstation is connected with the file server through a cable or T1 link using the IPX/SPX protocol. A user first logs in to a file server on a LAN and then establishes a communication session with a file server.

This type of link is set up by using REMOTE.NLM and RSPX.NLM at the file server and RCONSOLE at the workstation.

Asynchronous Link

In this method, a remote session is established using a modem. A user does not have to login to a file server. The user can use a standalone PC with a modem for the asynchronous link.

It is set up by using REMOTE.NLM and RS232.NLM at the file server and ACONSOLE at the remote workstation or PC.

Redundant Link

This method establishes redundant links, both direct and asynchronous, to the same file server.

Setting Up Remote Management

Hardware and Software Requirements

File Server Requirements

Hardware requirements for the file server:
- 386- or 486- microcomputer.
- 48KB of available memory to run NLMs.
- A Hayes-compatible modem (for an asynchronous link).

Software requirements for the file server:
- NetWare 3.0 or above.
- IPX/SPX network protocols.

Workstation Requirements

Hardware requirements for workstation:
- Novell-approved computer type and adapter board.
- At least 200KB of memory.
- A Hayes-compatible modem (for asynchronous connections).

Software requirements for the workstation:
- A workstation or standalone PC running DOS 2.x or above.

Using Direct Link Remote Management

Load the required NLMs on the file server as follows:

1. Load REMOTE

    (You will be prompted to enter a password. Users will be prompted to enter this password after selecting this file server for remote management).

2. Load RSPX

    You can run RCONSOLE from the workstation after loading the above NLMs. The "Available Server" screen will appear showing the name of the file server(s) that with REMOTE and RSPX loaded.

3. Next select the file server and enter the password (supervisor password will also work). An "Active File Server" screen will appear.

You can use the following keys for remote management:

- <-> or <+> keys on the number pad to move through the file server's active screens.
- <*> key on the number pad to bring up the remote management "Available Options" menu.
- <Esc> or <Alt><F10> to exit the menu.

Note: You must use the above keys on the keyboards numeric keypad. Other keys will not work. You also cannot use

<ALT><ESC> to move through the file server's screens, as you can from the file server.

RCONSOLE Menu Options

Available Options
Select A Screen To View
Directory Scan
Transfer Files To Server
Copy System and Public Files
Shell to Operating System
End Remote Session With Server (SHIFT-ESC)
Resume Remote Session With Server (ESC)

Figure 14-1 RCONSOLE Utility Screen.

Select Screen

This option lets you select the file server's active screens. If you want to load NLMs or use other console commands, select "System Console".

Directory Scan

Using this option, you can view files on the file server's local drives or on NetWare directories. For example if you want to view what is in the file server's DOS partition, enter C:. You can enter SYS:PUBLIC to view the PUBLIC directory. If you would like to edit any file, you can go to the system console and load EDIT.NLM to edit 8K or less text files:

> Load EDIT *filename*

Transfer Files to Server

Use this option to copy files to the file server's local drives or NetWare directories.

Copy System and Public Files

This option can be used to copy system and public files to the file server during remote installation or update. This option is only recommended for use with RCONSOLE. ACONSOLE is not recommended for transferring large files.

Shell to Operating System

Use this option to go to the operating system prompt. Type "EXIT" to return to the RCONSOLE menu.

End Remote Session With Server (SHIFT-ESC)

To end a remote session, select this option or press <Shift><Esc> or <Alt><F10>.

Resume Remote Session with Server

Select this option to exit from the "Available Options" menu or press <Esc> to exit.

Reboot a File Server from a Remote Console

To reboot a remote file server using RCONSOLE, run the following commands at the system console:

REMOVE DOS

DOWN

EXIT

When DOS is removed from memory, the EXIT command automatically performs a warm boot of the file server.

Make sure you have the following two lines in the AUTOEXEC.NCF file in addition to other lines, so that you can open a new remote session with the file server after rebooting:

LOAD REMOTE

LOAD RSPX

Review Questions

Q.1. Remote management allows you to _____ . (select the one that is not true)

   a. use Console commands from a workstation
   b. edit server's CONFIG.SYS file from a workstation
   c. transfer files from a remote server
   d. reboot a server from a workstation

Q.2. You can upgrade a NetWare server using remote management.

   a. true   b. false
   c. only 2.2   d. only 3.0 or above

Q.3. Which of the following can you not do using remote management?

   a. scan directories on the server
   b. transfer files to a remote server
   c. upgrade a 3.0 server
   d. create users

Q.4. What are the minimum rights you need to the SYS:SYSTEM directory to work as a console operator.

    a. RF   b. R

    c. S   d. RWF

Q.5. You must load _____ at the server for direct link remote management.

    a. REMOTE.NLM, and RSPX.NLM

    b. REMOTE.EXE, and RSPX.EXE

    c. REMOTE.NLM, and RS232.NLM

    d. REMOTE.NLM, and AUTOEXEC.NCF

Q.6. You use _____ at the workstation for direct link remote management.

    a. ACONSOLE.EXE   b. RCONSOLE.EXE

    c. RCONSOLE.NLM   d. SYSCON

Q.7. If a LAN driver is unloaded from the server, you would use _____ and _____ at the server and _____ at the workstation to load the LAN driver remotely.

    a. REMOTE, RSPX; RCONSOLE

    b. REMOTE, RS232; ACONSOLE

    c. REMOTE, RS232, RCONSOLE

    d. REMOTE, RSPX, ACONSOLE

Q.8. For remote console you use the _____ to move through the server's active screens.

    a. <-> or <+> key on the numeric keypad

    b. any <-> or <+> key on the keyboard

    c. <Alt> <Esc>

    d. <Alt> <F10>

Q.9. You use the _____ key on the numeric keypad to bring up the remote management menu.

    a. <*>   b. <F10>

    c. <-> or <+>   d. <F1>

Chapter 14: Remote Management

Q.10. The workstation must be at least a 386 computer to issue console commands using remote management.

    a. true   b. false

Q.11. The remote management facility (RMF) allows you to log in to the server as a remote user.

    a. true

    b. false

    c. only if you are a supervisor

    d. only if you are using asynchronous link

Q.12. To reboot a server from a remote console, issue the commands:

    a. REMOVE DOS, DOWN, EXIT

    b. EXIT, DOWN, REMOVE DOS

    c. REBOOT, REMOTE, DOWN

    d. REMOTE, RSPX, DOWN

Q.13. You can put LOAD REMOTE and LOAD RSPX commands in the _____ file to automatically enable remote management when the server is booted.

    a. CONFIG.SYS   b. AUTOEXEC.BAT

    c. AUTOEXEC.NCF   d. STARTUP.NCF

Chapter 15   Electronic Mail

Overview

Electronic Mail (E-Mail) has become a common place feature in the computer world. Novell now provides this service as an add-on to 3.11 or as a standard option with 3.12. It consists of three major components:

- Basic MHS (Message Handling Service) for routing messages at the file server.
- An Administration utility to maintain user database.
- First Mail user program to deal with writing and reading messages.

Basic MHS

Basic MHS is an entry level product to the world of E-Mail. It is limited to a single file server but is upwardly compatible to the more advanced Global MHS option from Novell.

Basic MHS can be installed on the file server during the original installation or as a later feature. The BASICMHS.NLM uses 250KB of file server memory and requires 2.5MB of disk space for programs and databases. It also requires the services of BTRIEVE v5.15 or later and CLIB 3.11e or later for database maintenance. It works with the Novell Standard Message Format (SMF).

Installation Process

1. Choose the Product Options Menu in INSTALL.

    Press the <Ins> key to add MHS.

2. Define the source path for the BASICMHS programs and auxiliaries of ADMIN and MAIL.

3. The major workgroup name defaults to the file server name on which MHS is installed. An alternate, such as organization name may be used. Basic MHS supports only one workgroup.

4. You can accept the default directory SYS:MHS to install files or specify another path.

5. The user list may be generated automatically from the bindery. This will make all network users MHS users. Users may be added or deleted later.

6. The address of the user is by default the long name of the user. The alternative is the login name.

    The installation software can add commands to the system login script to set a search mapping to MHS\EXE and an environment variable named "MV".

7. A directory for programs, users, and mailboxes is created and MAIL.EXE is added to SYS:PUBLIC.

8. An automatic update to the AUTOEXEC.NCF may be selected to add the SEARCH to the directory with BASICMHS.NLM and to load it on boot-up.

Basic MHS is recommended for use with systems that have 25 users or less.

Maintenance and Administration

The MHS is serviced by ADMIN.EXE that is in the SYS:MHS/EXE. Proper trustee rights to this directory should be made to ensure security. Since ADMIN.EXE requires BTRIEVE, BREQUEST.EXE must be run before ADMIN.EXE.

ADMIN has a main menu for the following actions:

1. Add, delete, and modify user accounts.
2. Establish named distribution lists for multi-addressing.
3. Register applications with access to the service.
4. Customize the configuration.

If a user is added through the ADMIN utility who was not added as a network user before, this user will be created as a network user. If you delete a user from MHS, it will not be deleted as a network user.

There is also an activity log BASICMHS.LOG that should be monitored in particular for any operation problems. This log will grow with usage and so it should be removed from the disk periodically.

Usage

The First Mail service for users is supplied by MAIL.EXE that will be installed in SYS:PUBLIC for access by DOS workstations. Novell also supplies a version for Macintosh workstations that would normally be installed at the workstation. Other E-Mail applications may also be used if they support the Standard Message Format (SMF). The DOS version requires 384K of workstation memory and suitable mapping to MHS/MAIL/USERS.

First Mail offers the usual E-Mail services for generating and sending messages, browsing mailboxes, saving messages in separate folders and recovering messages for edit and retransmission. It allows attachments, carbon copy addressing, forwarding, and return receipt.

The First Mail main menu offers the following options:

- N: Check for **N**ew mail
- S: **S**end a mail message
- B: **B**rowse mail messages
- P: **P**references
- E: **E**dit a file
- Q: **Q**uit using First Mail

Exercises

Administration

1. Login with the proper rights.
2. Run BREQUEST.
3. Run ADMIN.
4. Check the Users file for entries.
5. Add some MHS users.
6. If a user is added who has not been previously entered as a network user, use SYSCON to check if the user is added in the system.
7. Create a named distribution list with defined users.

Usage

1. Login as a user who is in the MHS database.
2. Generate a message to a single user. The MHS database may be checked using <F2> or you may type in a correct name.
3. Enter a subject to identify message.
4. Enter message and send <CTRL+ENTER>.
5. Generate a message using the named distribution list.
6. Login as a recipient and invoke mail to check mail.
7. Send another message with confirmation options accessed with <F9>.
8. Check to see whether delivery confirmation appears in your mail.

9. Login as a recipient and read the message.

10. Login as a sender to check read confirmation.

Review Questions

Q.1. The basic MHS bundled with NetWare 3.12 supports _____ file server(s).

    a. 1   b. 8

    c. 16   d. 250

Q.2. Basic MHS is automatically installed as a part of NetWare 3.12 installation.

    a. true   b. false

Q.3. Basic MHS is installed using the _____ .

    a. "Product Options" option in INSTALL.NLM

    b. "Copy System and Public Files" option in INSTALL.NLM

    c. INSTALL.EXE at the workstation

    d. BASICMHS.EXE at the server

Q.4. _____ is used to create MHS users.

    a. MAIL   b. ADMIN

    c. BASICMHS   d. INSTALL

Q.5. The _____ utility is used to create and send mail.

    a. MAIL   b. ADMIN

    c. BASICMHS   d. INSTALL

Final Hands-On Exercise

Congratulations! You are hired by a company to work as a LAN Administrator. Now you are supposed to do the following:

1. Login as a supervisor. Create yourself as a user and make yourself a Supervisor equivalent. Now logout and login using your name.

2. Install two applications on the network. Create a directory under APPS using your name. Install the applications under your directory. For example, if you are installing the application Quicken or Norton Commander they should be installed in the following directories:

    SYS:APPS\BOB\QUICKEN
    SYS:APPS\BOB\NC

    (Ask your instructor for the application disks.)

3. Check the attributes of files and change the attributes of .EXE files to Ro (read only) and S (shareable). Which two utilities can you use ?

    (1)_____. (2)_____.

4. Go to the work directory (SYS:APPS\WORK) and create a menu for your users. Use your name as menu name, e.g., BOBMENU.SRC. Your menu should have the same options as the sample menu in the NMENU chapter.

Change your options and executable lines according to your applications. You need a DOS (ASCII) editor to create menu script file (BOBMENU.SRC). What is the name of your editor? _____.

Where is it located? _____.

5. Create two users using your name like BOB1 and BOB2. Create their home directories under USERS like:

   SYS:USERS\BOB1
   SYS:USERS\BOB2

6. Create a login script for each user and do the following:

   - Search mapping to PUBLIC, DOS, and the applications directories.
   - Drive mapping H: to USERS (HOME) directory and J: to WORK directory.
   - Greeting message to users.
   - Default drive to J:
   - Exit to menu.

7. Login as a user BOB1. Do you see any error messages on screen? Why?

8. Make user BOB1's security equivalent to Supervisor. Which utility will you use? _____.

9. Give user BOB2 R W C E M F rights to the application directories. Which utilities can you use?

Final Hands-on Exercise

(1)_____. (2)_____.

10. Login as user BOB1 and then as user BOB2. Do you see any error messages now?

11. Create two more users BOB3 and BOB4. Login as BOB3 or BOB4 and try to run any application. You will see error messages on the screen.

    Make a group. Add these two users in this group. Give this group appropriate rights in the application directory. Now login again as BOB3 or BOB4 and try to run the application. Do you see error messages now?

Turnkey System

In a turnkey system, a user just boots the computer and is ready to use the applications. You can create a turnkey system by using the AUTOEXEC.BAT file, the login script, and the menu. The AUTOEXEC.BAT file contains commands that help the user to log in to the system. In the login script file, the user environment is set (drive and search mappings, etc.) and the menu program is called. The menu then allows users to execute applications just by selecting (pressing the <Enter> key) an option.

Create or modify your AUTOEXEC.BAT to include the following commands:

```
LSL
NE2000
```

IPXODI
VLM
F:

login username (replace username with your login name)

Make sure you are exiting to a menu in your login script. Now reboot your computer. You should be in your menu.

Printing Exercise

1. Using the PCONSOLE utility, create two queues, e.g.,

    QBOB_PANA and QBOB_HPIII

2. Assign queue QBOB_PANA to printer PANASONIC and queue QBOB_HPIII to printer HPIII.

3. Use the CAPTURE command to send your printing to both queues.

    For example:

    capture q=qBOB_pana nb ti=1

    You can print to the queues by using one of the following methods:

    Press PrintScrn key

    or

Final Hands-on Exercise

Send print jobs to LPT1 (local printer) by using DOS commands.

For example:

    DIR > PRN
    COPY AUTOEXEC.BAT PRN
    PRINT AUTOEXEC.BAT

All the above print jobs should go to the queue you specified with the CAPTURE command and should be printed on network printers.

4. Using the NPRINT command, print BOBMENU.SRC to both queues. BOBMENU.SRC should be in the APPS/WORK directory.

Managing Print Queues

1. Login as a Supervisor and run PCONSOLE.

2. Select your queue. Select "Current Queue Status" and change the Operator Flag "Servers can service entries in queue:" to NO (to stop printing from this queue).

3. Send three printing jobs using three different printing methods (NPRINT, Print Screen, PCONSOLE).

4. Select the queue and select the "Current Print Job Entries" option. The jobs you sent to print should be there. Now

select any job by pressing <Enter>. This displays the Print Queue Entry Information screen.

5. Go to different options and press <Enter> or press the <F1> key to get more information about the option.

6. Change the "Service Sequence:" for the last job. Type "yes" at User Hold option and see the change of Status.

7. Now change the queue status so that the jobs will print.

Steps to Control the Printer Using PCONSOLE

1. Run PCONSOLE.

2. Select Print Server Information and select Print Server.

3. Select Print Server Status/Control (This option will be available only if the print server is loaded).

4. Select Printer Status and select the printer.

5. Press <Enter> at the printer control to see the different options to control the printer. Press the <F1> key to get help.

6. Press <Enter> at the service mode to see different options.

APPENDIX A

Console Commands

ADD NAME SPACE	PROTOCOL
BIND	REGISTER MEMORY
BROADCAST	REMOVE DOS
CLEAR STATION	RESET ROUTER
CLS	SEARCH
CONFIG	SECURE CONSOLE
DISABLE LOGIN	SEND
DISABLE TTS	SET
DISMOUNT	SET TIME
DISPLAY NETWORKS	SPEED
DISPLAY SERVERS	SPOOL
DOWN	TIME
ENABLE LOGIN	TRACK OFF
ENABLE TTS	TRACK ON
EXIT	UNBIND
LOAD	UNLOAD
MEMORY	UPS STATUS
MODULES	UPS TIME
MOUNT	VERSION
NAME	VOLUMES
OFF	

Please refer to the Novell *System Administration* manual for full descriptions and command structures.

Command Line Utilities

ALLOW	NPRINT
ATOTAL	NVER
ATTACH	PAUDIT
BINDFIX	PSC
BINDREST	PURGE
CAPTURE	REMOVE
CASTOFF	RENDIR
CASTON	REVOKE
CHKDIR	RIGHTS
CHKVOL	RPRINTER
DOSGEN	SECURITY
ENDCAP	SEND
FLAG	SETPASS
FLAGDIR	SETTTS
GRANT	SLIST
LISTDIR	SMODE
LOGIN	SYSTIME
LOGOUT	TLIST
MAP	USERLIST
MENU	VERSION
NCOPY	WHOAMI
NDIR	WSUPDATE
NETBIOS	

Appendix A

Loadable Modules

CLIB	ROUTE
DISKSET	RS232
EDIT	RSPX
INSTALL	SPXCONFG
IPXS	SPXS
MATHLIB	STREAMS
MONITOR	TLI
NMAGENT	UPS
PSERVER	VREPAIR
REMOTE	

Menu Utilities

ACONSOLE	PRINTDEF
COLORPAL	RCONSOLE
DSPACE	SALVAGE
FCONSOLE	SESSION
FILER	SYSCON
MAKEUSER	USERDEF
PCONSOLE	VOLINFO
PRINTCON	

Command-Line Utilities Description

ALLOW

Used to view, set, or modify the Inherited Rights Mask (IRM) of a directory or a file.

ATOTAL

Used to total the accounting services usage on a network. Accounting services must be installed on the file server before you use this command.

ATTACH

Used to connect the workstation to multiple file servers.

BINDFIX

Used to correct problems with the NetWare bindery files.

BINDREST

Used to restore old versions of the bindery files after BINDFIX has been run.

CAPTURE

Used to print data to a network printer. The data may be screen dumps or data from an application that is not designed to run on networks.

CASTOFF

Used to block messages from other workstations.

CASTON

Used to allow the workstation to receive messages again from other network users after CASTOFF has been used.

CHKDIR

Used to view information about a directory and a volume.

CHKVOL

Used to view information about a particular volume.

COMCHECK

Used to test the communication between the file server and workstations.

DCONFIG

Used to change the IPX.COM file to match the setting on the network board.

DOSGEN

This utility allows the DOS workstation to boot from the file server rather than from a boot diskette in a local drive.

ECONFIG

Used to configure the workstation shells to use the Ethernet II Standard.

EMSNETx

Used to load the NetWare Expanded Memory Shell at the workstation. The " x " represents the DOS version.

ENDCAP

Used to close a spooled file and send the data from the spooled file to the printer.

FLAG

Used to view and change the file attributes.

FLAGDIR

Used to view and change the directory attributes.

GRANT

Used to grant trustee rights to users or groups in a file or a directory.

HELP

This utility displays on-line information about using NetWare utilities.

IPX

This utility loads the Internetwork Packet eXchange protocol.

LISTDIR

Used to view the directory structure of a specified volume, drive or directory.

LOGIN

This utility allows the user to log in to the network.

LOGOUT

This utility logs the user out of one or all file servers.

MAP

Used to view or assign drive mappings.

MENU

Used to access customized menus that users create.

NCOPY

This utility copies files from one location to another.

NDIR

Used to specify exactly the set of files the user wants to view in a directory.

NETX

This utility loads the NetWare shell at the workstation.

NETBIOS

Used to view NetWare version information, whether NETBIOS is loaded, and which interrupts are in use, and to unload NETBIOS.

NPRINT

Used to print ASCII text files.

NVER

This utility lists the current version of NetWare, NetBIOS, IPX, SPX, and the LAN driver.

PAUDIT

Used to view the system accounting records.

PSC

Used to view the status of the print servers and network printers. It allows the user to issue commands to the print server from the command line, rather than from PCONSOLE.

PURGE

Used to permanently delete the previously erased files.

REMOVE

Used to delete a user or a group from the trustee list of a file or a directory.

RENDIR

Used to rename a directory.

REVOKE

Used to revoke trustee rights from a user or group in a file or directory.

RIGHTS

This utility can be used by the user to view his effective rights in a file or a directory.

RPRINTER

Used to connect or disconnect a remote printer from a print server.

SECURITY

Used to view possible file server security violations.

SEND

Used to send one-line messages from one workstation to another workstation or group.

SETPASS

Used to create or change the password on one or more file servers.

SETTTS

Used to ensure that the Transaction Tracking System (TTS) is working.

SLIST

Used to list all the file servers connected to the internetwork.

SMODE

Used to specify how a program will use search drives when looking for a data file.

SYSTIME

Used to view the server time. It also synchronizes the local workstation time with that of the file servers.

TLIST

Used to view the trustee list of a directory or a file.

USERLIST

Used to list the users currently logged into the file server.

VERSION

Used to view the version of a NetWare utility.

WHOAMI

Used to display your user name, the file server's name, software version, the date and time of login, the group you belong to, your rights, and security equivalences.

WSGEN

Used to create the IPX.COM program used with NETx.COM to connect a workstation to a file server.

WSUPDATE

This utility updates workstation files from the file server. It should be run from the system login script.

XMSNETx

Used to load the NetWare Extended Memory Shell at the workstation. The " x " represents the DOS version.

Menu Utilities Description

ACONSOLE

Used for remote management using an asynchronous link. It controls the transfer of screen and keystroke information to and from the remote file server.

COLORPAL

Used to paint a color scheme on the user's menu screen.

DSPACE

Used to limit the user's disk space on a volume and in a directory and to limit disk space in a directory.

FCONSOLE

Used to down the server, broadcast messages, view the current user connection information, view the version of NetWare, and change the status of the file server.

FILER

Used to manage volumes, directories, and files, and to change directory and file security.

JUMPERS

Used to configure the IPX LAN driver to match the network board settings.

MAKEUSER

Used by the supervisor or the workgroup manager to create or delete users by creating script files (.USR files).

PCONSOLE

This is the main utility for print management. It can be used to setup print servers, create queues, control network printing, and view information about network printing.

PRINTCON

Used to define preferred print options and save them as configuration files.

PRINTDEF

Used to set up a database of printer definitions and to define forms.

RCONSOLE

Used to access a file server from a workstation for remote management using the direct link method.

SALVAGE

Used to recover deleted files that have not been purged.

SESSION

Used to create, change, and delete drive mappings.

SYSCON

Used to control accounting, to manage users and groups, and to assign users' rights, etc. More than 80% of administrative tasks are usually done using SYSCON utility.

UPGRADE

Used to upgrade the bindery, data and security on the NetWare 2.x file server to a 3.x format.

USERDEF

Used by the supervisor or workgroup manager to create users by using templates.

VOLINFO

Used to view information about each volume on a file server.

APPENDIX B

Directory Structure

Important Directories and Files:

Volume:
    <Directory>
        <<Sub-directory>>
            <<<Sub-directory>>>
                Files

SYS:

        TTS$LOG.ERR
        VOL$LOG.ERR
        DELETED.SAV
        BACKOUT.TTS

    SYS:LOGIN

        LOGIN.EXE
        SLIST.EXE
        TOKEN.RPL

SYS:SYSTEM

AUTOEXEC.NCF
NET$OBJ.SYS
NET$PROP.SYS
NET$VAL.SYS
WANGTEK.NLM
TSA311.NLM

SYS:SYSTEM\xxxx.QDR

xxxxxxxx.SRV
xxxxxxxx.SYS

SYS:SYSTEM\DIBI

DIBI2$DV.DAT

SYS:PUBLIC

xxxxxxxx.PDF
NET$PRN.DAT
NET$LOG.DAT
PCONSOLE.EXE
PRINTCON.EXE
PRINTDEF.EXE
PSC.EXE
RPRINTER.EXE
SALVAGE.EXE
SYS$ERR.DAT
TOKEN.RPL
WANGTEK.EXE

Appendix B

SYS:MAIL

    SYS:MAIL\USER_ID

        LOGIN
        PRINTCON.DAT
        LOGIN.OS2

SYS:ETC

    SYS:ETC\SAMPLES

        GATEWAYS
        HOSTS
        NETWORKS
        PROTOCOL
        SERVICES

SYS:USERS

    SYS:USERS\<USER'S NAME>

SYS:APPS

    SYS:APPS\CLIPPER5
    SYS:APPS\DBASE
    SYS:APPS\DBWD
    SYS:APPS\DOS
    SYS:APPS\NC
    SYS:APPS\QUICKEN
    SYS:APPS\UTILITY
    SYS:APPS\WINDOWS
    SYS:APPS\WINWORD

© 1993 - 95 · PC Age, Inc. All Rights Reserved · 20 Audrey Place · Fairfield, NJ 07004 · U.S.A. · Tel: 201-882-5370

Multiple-Choice Practice Questions

Q.1. Which is not linked to the operating system?

    a. NLM   c. Disk Drivers

    b. LAN Drivers   d. Management Utilities

Q.2. Which Rights are needed to run MENU when the menu file is not in the current directory?

    a. RFA   b. RF

    c. RCMF   d. RCMFEW

Q.3. What can run on a file server to provide printing services?

    a. PSERVER.NLM   c. PSERVER.EXE

    b. PCONSOLE.NLM   d. PRINTDEF.EXE

Q.4. Which utility modifies the IRM of a directory ?

    a. GRANT   c. ALLOW

    b. RIGHTS   d. SESSION

Q.5. What are the default rights for the group EVERYONE in the PUBLIC directory ?

    a. C   b. RF

    c. R F C   d. none of the above

Q.6. When in a login script, which command is used to get the MYMENU program to run?

    a. Exit "MENU MYMENU.MNU"

    b. Exit "NMENU MYMENU"

    c. # MENU MYMENU.MNU

    d. MENU MYMENU.MNU

Q.7. What rights are needed to execute an .EXE file?

    a. RF   b. RWC

    c. RFA   d. RWECM

Q.8. If you wanted to grant a user rights to copy a file from one directory to another what is the correct syntax?

    a. GRANT W C F FOR G: TO USER BOB

    b. GRANT FOR G: W C F TO USER BOB

    c. GRANT USER W C F FOR G:

d. ALLOW W C F TO USER BOB

Q.9. Which attribute is used for both files and directories?

    a. H   b. R

    c. E   d. A

Q.10. What information does WHOAMI not give you?

    a. File server name   c. Login time

    b. NetWare version   d. Node address

Q.11. The SECURITY command lets you?

    a. Change rights

    b. Change attributes

    c. See security holes in your system

    d. Change password

Q.12. Which command is used with quotes in a login script to display text?

    a. #   c. DISPLAY

    b. WRITE   d. FDISPLAY

Q.13. Which shell takes advantage of expanded memory?

    a. XMSNETx.EXE   c. NETx.COM

    b. EMSNETx.EXE   d. IPX.COM

Q.14. Which utility is used to change IRMs?

    a. SYSCON   c. PCONSOLE

    b. FILER   d. USERDEF

Q.15. Which allows you to create a template for a user?

    a. MAKEUSER   c. SYSCON

    b. USERDEF   d. PCONSOLE

Q.16. The EMSNETx.EXE uses which of the following?

    a. NetWare 3.12   c. NETx v.1

    b. NetWare 2.2   d. LIM 4.0

Q.17. Which files are in the LOGIN directory?

    a. SLIST.EXE, LOGIN.EXE

    b. SYSCON.EXE, LOGIN.EXE

    c. IPX.COM, NETx.COM

d. NET$LOG.DAT, LOGIN.EXE

Q.18. Which locks the file server console for security?

    a. SECURITY   c. MONITOR.NLM

    b. SECURE CONSOLE   d. LOCK.NLM

Q.19. When you are in SYSCON, which key would you press to rename a user name?

    a. Insert   b. F3

    c. F1   d. F5

Q.20. WSUPDATE should be run from?

    a. User Login Script   c. System Login Script

    b. Workstation   d. File server

Q.21. Where should you put the Exit command in the SYSTEM login script if you want to run user login scripts?

    a. Beginning of the login script

    b. Middle of the login script

    c. End of the login script

    d. None of the above

Q.22. How will you check from the command line that your menu is working?

    a. #NMENU MYMENU

    b. NMENU MYMENU

    c. EXIT "NMENU MYMENU"

    d. None of the above

Q.23. What is the file name of the system login script?

    a. NET$DOS.SYS   c. LOGIN.SYS

    b. NET$LOG.SYS   d. NET$LOG.DAT

Q.24. The system login script is stored in which directory?

    a. Public   b. System

    c. Apps   d. Mail

Q.25. Printer Sequence codes are in files with extensions_____ and these files are stored in the directory _____?

    a. .PDF, system   c. .DAT, public

    b. .PDF, public   d. .DAT, mail

Q.26. INSTALL.NLM is stored in which directory?

    a. Public   b. System

    c. Mail   d. Login

Q.27. When you create a new file in a network, it has which attributes?

    a. RW, A   b. RO, S

    c. RW, S, A   d. RO, S, A

Q.28. The NETBIOS statement is stored in the file?

    a. AUTOEXEC.BAT   c. CONFIG.SYS

    b. SHELL.CFG   d. NET.CFG

Q.29. Which is the right way to delete a map?

    a. MAP del g: c. del MAP g:

    b. del g: d. rem MAP g:

Q.30. The NetWare log has what?

    a. Technical Information

    b. SYSTEM Information

c. Error Messages

d. Troubleshooting techniques

Q.31. NetWire can be used to do what?

    a. Down load files and technical information

    b. Get technical support

    c. Novell Product and Service Information

    d. All of the above

Q.32. NetWare Buyer's Guide can be used for what?

    a. Novell Product Information

    b. Troubleshooting techniques

    c. SYSTEM Information

    d. All of the above

Answers

(1). d   (2). b   (3). a   (4). c   (5). b

(6). b   (7). a   (8). a   (9). a   (10). d

(11). c   (12). b   (13). b   (14). b   (15). b

(16). d   (17). a   (18). c   (19). b   (20). c

(21). d   (22). b   (23). d   (24). a   (25). b

(26). b   (27). a   (28). c   (29). a   (30). b

(31). d   (32). a

Answers to Review Questions

Chapter 1

(1). a   (2). b   (3). a   (4). d   (5). c

Chapter 2

(1). c   (2). c   (3). b

Chapter 3

(1). a   (2). a   (3). c   (4). a   (5). c

Chapter 4

(1). a   (2). c   (3). d   (4). b   (5). b

(6). a   (7). a   (8). a, c

Chapter 5

(1). a   (2). a   (3). c   (4). a   (5). b

© 1993 - 95 · PC Age, Inc. All Rights Reserved · 20 Audrey Place · Fairfield, NJ 07004 · U.S.A. · Tel: 201-882-5370

(6). a   (7). b   (8). b

Chapter 6

(1). c, d   (2). c   (3). a   (4). b   (5). c

(6). a   (7). a   (8). d

Chapter 7

(1). b   (2). a, c   (3). c   (4). a   (5). c

(6). b   (7). b   (8). b   (9). b   (10). b   (11). d

Chapter 8

(1). a   (2). a   (3). b   (4). b   (5). c

(6). c

Chapter 9

(1). a   (2). a   (3). b   (4). b   (5). c

(6). a, d   (7). a   (8). a, c   (9). b   (10). a

(11). d   (12). d   (13). a   (14). c   (15). d

(16). a   (17). b

Chapter 10

(1). a   (2). b   (3). d   (4). a,c   (5). c

(6). a   (7). b   (8). c   (9). d

Chapter 11

(1). c, d   (2). c   (3). d

Chapter 12

(1). b   (2). c   (3). b   (4). c

Chapter 13

(1). b   (2). a   (3). b   (4). b   (5). b

(6). c   (7). b   (8). e   (9). d   (10). d

(11). b   (12). a   (13). a   (14). a   (15). d

(16). a   (17). a   (18). b   (19). a   (20). c

Chapter 14

(1). c (2). d (3). d (4). a (5). a

(6). b (7). b (8). a (9). a (10). b

(11). b (12). a (13). c

Chapter 15

(1). a (2). b (3). a (4). b (5). a

INDEX

A

#	9-2
A Simple Sample Menu	10-2
ACONSOLE.EXE	14-4
Administration	15-5
ALL	13-13
ALLOW	7-18
Answer to Exercise 7.1.	7-24
Application Directory	4-7
Assigning Print Queues to Printers	13-5
Asynchronous Link	14-5
ATTACH	9-3
Attribute Security	7-11
AUTOEXEC.BAT	8-7

B

Backup Responsibilities	12-3
Basic MHS	15-1
BREAK ON/OFF	9-4

C

CAncel	13-13
CancelALL	13-13
CancelLocal=n	13-13
CAPTURE Options	13-11
Central Processing	1-2
CHKDIR	4-21
CHKVOL	4-15
Client	1-2
Command Line Utilities	3-1
Communication Link Types	14-5
Communication Protocol	8-2
Compatibility with Earlier Versions	10-10
Compiling Menus	10-9
COMSPEC	9-4
CONFIG.SYS	8-7
Connecting a Workstation	8-1
Console Commands	3-9
Console Operator	6-3
Control Commands	10-4
Copy System and Public Files	14-10
Copying Directories and Files using the NCOPY Command	4-24
Creating a Print Server Account and Defining Printers	13-4
Creating Directories on the Server	4-10
Creating Queues	13-4

D

Default Login Script	9-2
Deleting A Mapping	5-8
Differential Backup	12-2
Direct Link	14-5
Directories	4-18
Directories You Should Create on the Server	4-5
Directory Scan	14-9
Disadvantages	4-9
Disk Mirroring and Duplexing	2-2
DISPLAY	9-4
Distributed Network Management	6-2
Distributed Processing	1-2
DOS BREAK ON/OFF	9-5
DOS Directories	4-7
DOS SET	9-5
DOS VERIFY ON/OFF	9-5
DRIVE	9-5
Drive Mappings	5-1
DSPACE	4-21
Duplicate DETs and FATs	2-1

E

Effective Packet Signature of Server and Workstation	7-23
Effective Rights	7-8

© 1993 - 95 · PC Age, Inc. All Rights Reserved · 20 Audrey Place · Fairfield, NJ 07004 · U.S.A. · Tel: 201-882-5370

END REMOTE SESSION WITH SERVER (SHIFT-ESC)	14-10	INSTALL	3-10
ENDING THE CAPTURE COMMAND	13-12	INSTALLATION PROCESS	15-2
EXECUTING MENUS	10-9	INSTALLING APPLICATIONS ON A NETWORK	11-1
EXERCISE 7.1:	7-11	INSTALLING WORKSTATION SOFTWARE	8-9
EXERCISES	15-5		
EXIT	9-6		

J

F

FDISPLAY	9-6		
FILE AND DIRECTORY ATTRIBUTES	7-12		
FILE SERVER REQUIREMENTS	14-6		
FILE SERVER SECURITY	7-16		
FILE SERVER SOFTWARE FOR REMOTE MANAGEMENT	14-3		
FILE SERVER UTILITIES	3-9		
FILER	4-15	LISTDIR	4-16
FILES	4-17	LOADING PSERVER.EXE ON DEDICATED WORKSTATION	13-6
FIRE PHASERS	9-7	LOADING PSERVER.NLM ON THE FILE SERVER	13-6
FLAG	7-19	LOADING THE PRINT SERVER PROGRAM	13-6
FLAGDIR	7-19	LOCAL=N	13-13
		LOGIN SCRIPT COMMANDS	9-2
		LOGIN/PASSWORD RESTRICTIONS	7-1

K

L

G

GOTO	9-7		
GRANT	7-18		
GROUPS	6-1		

M

MACHINE	9-9
MAINTENANCE AND ADMINISTRATION	15-3
MAKEUSER	6-11
MAKEUSER AND USERDEF	6-11
MAKEUSER KEYWORDS	6-12
MANAGING DELETED FILES WITH SALVAGE AND PURGE	4-25
MANAGING FILES WITH THE FILER UTILITY	4-24
MAP	9-9
MENU UTILITIES	3-1
MONITOR	3-10
MULTIPLE VOLUME SERVER	4-8

H

HANDS-ON EXERCISE	5-12
HANDS-ON EXERCISES	4-28
HARDWARE AND SOFTWARE REQUIREMENTS	14-6
HARDWARE REQUIREMENTS FOR THE FILE SERVER:	14-6
HARDWARE REQUIREMENTS FOR WORKSTATION:	14-6
HOME DIRECTORIES	4-6

I

N

IF...THEN...ELSE	9-8	NCP PACKET SIGNATURE	7-20
IMPORTANT MANAGEMENT NLM UTILITIES	3-10	NDIR	4-17
INCLUDE	9-9	NET.CFG	8-8
INCREMENTAL BACKUP	12-2	NETWARE DIRECTORY STRUCTURE	4-1
		NETWARE DOS REQUESTER	8-1

Index

NetWare GUI Utilities	3-2	Redundant Link	14-5
NetWare Loadable Modules (NLMs)	3-9	REMARK	9-11
NetWare Print Server	13-1	Remote Booting	3-11
NetWare Supervisor	14-2	Remote Console Operator	14-2
NetWare 3.12 Rights	7-4	Remote Printer Software	13-2
NetWare Volumes	4-1	REMOTE.NLM	14-3
NetWare-Created Directories	4-3	REMOVE	7-19
Network	1-1	Removing a Directory Using the FILER Utility	4-12
Network Drive Mapping	5-3	RENDIR	4-22
Network Drives	5-1	Restore Strategies	12-2
Network Printing from MS Windows	13-14	Resume Remote Session with Server	14-10
Network Printing Steps	13-4	Review Questions	1-4
Network Printing Users	13-18	Review Questions	2-3
Networking Basics	1-1	Review Questions	3-12
NO_DEFAULT	9-10	Review Questions	4-26
Novell Supplied Services	12-3	Review Questions	5-9
NPRINT Options	13-14	Review Questions	6-23
		Review Questions	7-25
		Review Questions	8-10
		Review Questions	9-16

O

Open Data-Link Interface (ODI)	8-3	Review Questions	10-12
Organizational Commands	10-2	Review Questions	11-3
Other Attributes	7-15	Review Questions	12-6
Overview	10-1	Review Questions	13-19
Overview	12-1	Review Questions	14-12
Overview	15-1	Review Questions	15-7
		REVOKE	7-18
		RIGHTS	7-20
		Rights Requirements	7-6
		Rights Security	7-3
		RS232.NLM	14-3

P

PAUSE	9-10	RSPX.NLM	14-3
PCCOMPATIBLE	9-10	Running RPRINTER	13-7
PCONSOLE	13-3		
Preparing a Menu	10-1		
PRINTCON	13-17		
PRINTDEF	13-17	## S	
Printing on a Network	13-1		
PURGE	4-25	SALVAGE	4-25
		Sample NDIR Screen	4-19
		Sample System and User Login Scripts	9-14

Q

		SBACKUP Process	12-4
		Search Drive Mapping	5-5
		Search Drives	5-5
		Search Mappings and the DOS PATH Environment	5-6

R

		Security Levels	7-1
RCONSOLE Menu Options	14-9	Select Screen	14-9
RCONSOLE.EXE	14-4	Server	1-1
Read-After-Write Verification	2-1	Server Levels	7-21
Reboot a File Server from a Remote Console	14-11	Setting Up Remote Management	14-6
		Shared Data Area	4-7

© 1993 - 95 · PC Age, Inc. All Rights Reserved · 20 Audrey Place · Fairfield, NJ 07004 · U.S.A. · Tel: 201-882-5370

SHELL TO OPERATING SYSTEM	14-10	USING ELECTROTEXT	3-7
SHIFT	9-11	USING REMOTE MANAGEMENT	14-2
SLIST	4-11	USING SECURITY-RELATED NETWARE	
SOFTWARE REQUIREMENTS FOR THE FILE SERVER:	14-6	COMMANDS	7-18
		USING THE DSPACE UTILITY	4-29
SOFTWARE REQUIREMENTS FOR THE WORKSTATION:	14-6	USING THE NETWARE FILER UTILITY TO CREATE DIRECTORIES	4-11
SOFTWARE TO CONNECT A DOS WORKSTATION	8-5	USING THE SALVAGE UTILITY	4-29
		USING USER TOOLS	3-4
SOURCE COMMANDS	10-2	UTILITIES FOR CREATING USERS AND GROUPS	6-5
SOURCE ROUTING SUPPORT	3-11		
SPOOL (CONSOLE COMMAND)	13-16	UTILITIES USED FOR VIEWING SERVER INFORMATION	4-11
STATION, TIME, AND OTHER ACCOUNT RESTRICTIONS	7-2	UTILITIES USED FOR VIEWING VOLUME INFORMATION	4-15
STRATEGIES FOR BACKUP AND RESTORE	12-1		
SUBDIRECTORIES	4-18	UTILITIES USED TO VIEW OR CHANGE INFORMATION ABOUT DIRECTORIES	4-16
SUPPORTING WINDOWS WORKSTATIONS	8-9		
SYSTEM FAULT TOLERANT CAPABILITIES	2-1		
SYSTEM LOGIN SCRIPT	9-1		
SYSTEM LOGIN SCRIPT	9-14	**V**	
		VOLINFO	4-15

T

THE CAPTURE COMMAND	13-11	**W**	
THE INHERITED RIGHTS MASK (IRM)	7-7		
THE NETWARE BINDERY	7-17	WHAT USER ACCOUNT MANAGERS CAN DO	6-3
THE NPRINT COMMAND	13-14		
THE SYSCON UTILITY	6-5	WHAT USER ACCOUNT MANAGERS CAN'T DO	6-3
TLIST	7-20		
TRANSACTION TRACKING SYSTEM (TTS)	2-2	WHAT WORKGROUP MANAGERS CAN DO	6-2
TRUSTEE RIGHTS ASSIGNMENTS	7-7	WHAT WORKGROUP MANAGERS CAN'T DO	6-2
TYPES OF LOGIN SCRIPTS	9-1	WORKGROUP MANAGER	6-2
		WORKSTATION CONFIGURATION FILES	8-7
U		WORKSTATION ENVIRONMENTS SUPPORTED BY NETWARE 3.12	1-3
UNDERSTANDING DRIVE MAPPINGS	5-12	WORKSTATION LEVELS	7-22
UNDERSTANDING LOGGING IN	4-28	WORKSTATION REQUIREMENTS	14-6
UNDERSTANDING THE DIRECTORY STRUCTURE	4-28	WORKSTATION SOFTWARE FOR REMOTE MANAGEMENT	14-4
UPS MONITORING	2-2	WORKSTATION UTILITIES	3-1
USAGE	15-4	WRITE	9-12
USAGE	15-5		
USER ACCOUNT MANAGER	6-3		
USER LOGIN SCRIPT	9-2	**X**	
USER LOGIN SCRIPT	9-15		
USERDEF	6-21		
USERS	6-1	**Y**	
USING DIRECT LINK REMOTE MANAGEMENT	14-7		
USING DOS TO CREATE DIRECTORIES	4-10	**Z**	

© 1993 - 95 · PC Age, Inc. All Rights Reserved · 20 Audrey Place · Fairfield, NJ 07004 · U.S.A. · Tel: 201-882-5370

Now You Can Prepare for All 7 Tests to Become a Novell CNE Right on Your PC

CNE CBT™
(Computer Based Training)
for Win/Win95/NT

- Complete course material for all 7 tests
- CNE TestMaster includes hundreds of multiple choice practice questions
- NetWare Interactive Simulator teaches you NetWare by hands-on exercises
- NSEPro and MTL hands-on exercises
- Novell Networking Glossary contains over 1100 terms and commands of NetWare
- Complete material for your home-study needs for Novell CNE

Best Buy

If you want to become a **Certified Novell Engineer (CNE)** and need complete material for the preparation with convenience and flexibility, you need CNE CBT (Computer Based Training). This one CD-ROM provides you with all the material you need to become a Novell CNE. You can easily carry it with you to practice either at home or at the office.

CNE CBT contains all test preparation material from our CNE Training Manuals on CD-ROM in CBT format. There are exercises at the end of chapters allowing you to check your knowledge and understanding. Furthermore, there are hundreds of multiple choice practice questions as covered in CNE TestMaster to practice for the actual Novell tests. In addition, there are over 50 hands-on exercises for either 3.1x or 4.11 track from NetWare Interactive Simulator. You can learn through real hands-on experience with NetWare even if you don't have NetWare available.

Novell Networking Glossary helps you in searching for terms and commands used in NetWare and gives you a brief description of each. In short, CNE CBT is the complete solution for your CNE home-study needs.

System Requirements: 486+ PC, Windows 3.1+, 8 MB RAM, 4x CD-ROM Drive, 10 MB hard disk space.

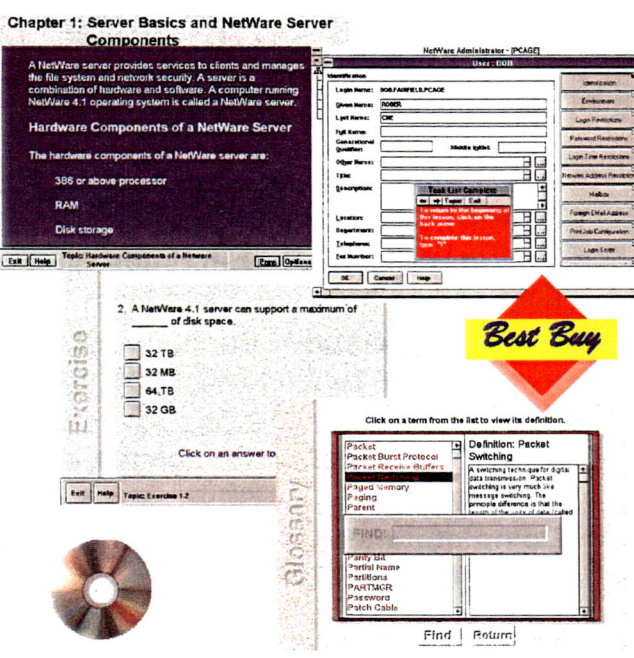

This is Absolutely, Positively, the ONLY thing you need to become a Novell CNE!

3.1x Track Covers the Following Novell Tests
Course 508, Administration 3.12
Course 518, Advanced Administration 3.12
Course 802, Installation & Configuration Workshop 3.12
Course 526, NetWare 3.1x to 4.11 Update
Course 801, Service & Support
Course 200, Networking Technologies
Course 605, NetWare TCP/IP Transport (elective)

4.11 Track Covers the Following Novell Tests
Course 520, Administration 4.11
Course 525, Advanced Administration 4.11
Course 804, Installation & Configuration Workshop 4.11
Course 532, Design and Implementation 4.11
Course 540, Building Intranets with IntranetWare 4.11
Course 801, Service & Support
Course 200, Networking Technologies

CNE CBT 3.1x Track Item No. CBT312-797 ....$995
CNE CBT 4.11 Track Item No. CBT411-797 ....$995
CNE CBT <u>both</u> 3.1x & 4.11 Tracks (one CD) $1195
Item No. CBT31411-797
5 User Version $2995. 10 User Version $4995. 25+ User, Call.
(shipped in CD-ROM only)

Ask for Special Upgrade Prices

Order Today!!! 1-800-PCAGE-60 (1-800-722-4360)
PC Age, Inc.: 20 Audrey Place, Fairfield, NJ 07004. U.S.A. International: (01) 732-287-3622, Fax: (01) 732-287-4511
Visit us on the WEB at: http://www.pcage.com or E-Mail: sales@pcage.com

Effective 07/21/97

This is Absolutely, Positively, the ONLY thing you need to become a Novell CNA!

CNA CBT (Computer Based Training) for Win/Win95/NT

- Complete course material for the CNA tests
- One CD-ROM covers both CNA 3 & CNA 4
- TestMaster includes hundreds of multiple choice practice questions
- NetWare Interactive Simulator teaches you NetWare by hands-on exercises
- Novell Networking Glossary contains over 1100 terms and commands of NetWare
- Complete material for your home-study needs for Novell CNA

If you want to become a Certified Novell Administrator (CNA) and need complete material for the preparation with convenience and flexibility, you need CNA CBT (Computer Based Training). This one CD-ROM provides you with all the material you need to become a Novell CNA. You can easily carry it with you to practice either at home or at the office.

CNA Computer Based Training contains all test preparation material from our Training Manuals. There are exercises at the end of each chapter allowing you to check your knowledge and understanding. Furthermore, there are hundreds of multiple choice practice questions as covered in TestMaster to practice for the actual Novell tests. In addition, there are hands-on exercises from NetWare Interactive Simulator. You can learn through real hands-on experience with NetWare even if you don't have NetWare available.

Novell Networking Glossary helps you in searching for terms and commands used in NetWare and gives you a brief description of each. In short, CNA Computer Based Training is the complete solution for your CNA home-study needs.

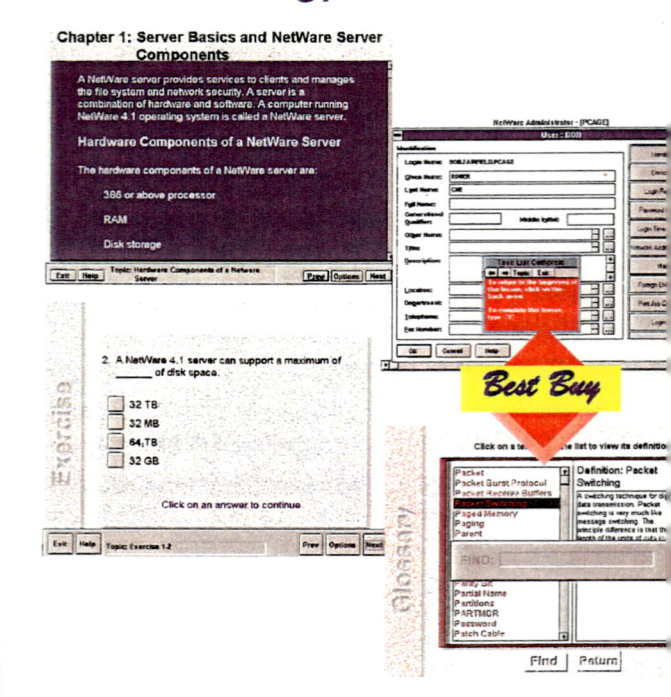

Now You Can Prepare to Become a Novell CNA Right on Your PC

CNA CBT Covers the Following Novell Tests
Novell course 508, Administration 3.1x, Certified Novell Administrator CNA/CNE test #50-130.

Novell course 520, Administration 4.11, Certified Novell Administrator CNA/CNE test #50-613.

CNA CBT for <u>both</u> 3.1x & 4.11 Tracks (one CD) Item No. CNACBT34-797	......$395
5 User Version Item No. 5CNACBT34-797	.....$1195
10 User Version Item No. 10CNACBT34-797 (shipped in CD-ROM only)	.....$1995

Ask for Special Upgrade Price

System Requirements: 486+ PC, Windows 3.1+, MB RAM, 4x CD-ROM Drive, 10 MB Hard Disk space

---

Order Today!!! 1-800-PCAGE-60 (1-800-722-4360)

PC Age, Inc.: 20 Audrey Place, Fairfield, NJ 07004. U.S.A. International: (01) 732-287-3622, Fax: (01) 732-287-4511
Visit us on the WEB at: http://www.pcage.com or E-Mail: sales@pcage.com

Effective 08/01/

Conquer Your CNE Exams With These Comprehensive Training Manuals

CNE Training Manuals

- Concise, to-the-point, up-to-date, and easy to understand
- Covers all 7 CNE tests for either 3.1x or 4.11
- Used in training institutes all over the world including colleges and universities
- Great as reference manuals for NetWare LAN administration tasks
- Rated "excellent" by hundreds of students

Rated Excellent

These Training Manuals are not designed only for test preparation, they are teaching manuals and being used in training centers all over the world.

To study at home to become a Certified Novell Engineer (CNE) you need these CNE Training Manuals. They cover what you need to know to pass the exams required to become a CNE. In addition, these manuals are great as a reference for NetWare LAN Administration tasks. Choose either NetWare 3.12 or NetWare 4.11 manuals, or both, depending on the certification you want.

4.11 Track Covers the Following Novell Tests

"System Administration v4.11" for Novell course 520, Administration v4.11, CNE/CNA test #50-613.
Item No. SA411-613 ..... $100

"Advanced System Administration v4.11" for Novell course 525, Advanced Administration v4.11, test #50-614. **Item No. ASA411-614** $100

"Installing & Configuring NetWare v4.11" for Novell course 804, NetWare v4.11 Installation & Configuration Workshop, test #50-617. **Item No. IC411-617** $100

"Designing NetWare v4.11" for Novell course 532, NetWare v4.11 Design & Implementation, test #50-601. **Item No. DI41-601** $100

For Novell course 540, Building Intranets with IntranetWare test #50-627.
Item No. BII411-627 ..... $100

"Data Communication & Networking Concepts" for Novell course 200, Networking Technologies, test #50-147.
Item No. NT-147 ..... $100

"Troubleshooting & Supporting Networks" for Novell course 801, NetWare Service & Support, test #50-602.
Item No. SS-602 ..... $100

All Seven Training Manuals for 4.11 Track
Item No. CSG411-797 ~~$700~~ **$495**

3.1x Track Covers the Following Novell Tests

"System Administration v3.12" for Novell course 508, Administration v3.1x, CNE/CNA test #50-130.
Item No. SA312-130 .... $75

"Advanced System Administration v3.12" for Novell course 518, Advanced Administration v3.1x, test #50-131. **Item No. ASA312-131** $75

"Installing & Configuring NetWare v3.1x" for Novell course 802, NetWare v3.1x Installation & Configuration Workshop, test #50-132. **Item No. IC312-132** $75

"NetWare v3.1x to NetWare v4.11 Update" for Novell course 526, NetWare 3.1x to 4.11 Update, test #50-615.
Item No. UD3141-615 ..... $100

"Data Communication & Networking Concepts" for Novell course 200, Networking Technologies, test #50-147.
Item No. NT-147 ..... $100

"Troubleshooting & Supporting Networks" for Novell course 801, NetWare Service & Support, test #50-602.
Item No. SS-602 ..... $100

"NetWare TCP/IP Support" for Novell course 605, NetWare TCP/IP Transport, test #50-145 (elective). **Item No. TCPIP-145** $100

All Seven Training Manuals for 3.1x Track
Item No. CSG312-797 ~~$625~~ **$450**

"I just wanted to let you know that I did not miss a single question on the exam. I want to thank you and everyone else that works at PC Age for the incredible customer service, and for the great test preparation material."

Order Today!!! 1-800-PCAGE-60 (1-800-722-4360)

PC Age, Inc.: 20 Audrey Place, Fairfield, NJ 07004. U.S.A. International: (01) 732-287-3622, Fax: (01) 732-287-4511
Visit us on the WEB at: http://www.pcage.com or E-Mail: sales@pcage.com

Effective 07/21/97

Learn NetWare with Hands-On Training Without Installing NetWare!

NetWare *Interactive* Simulator
for Win/Win95/NT

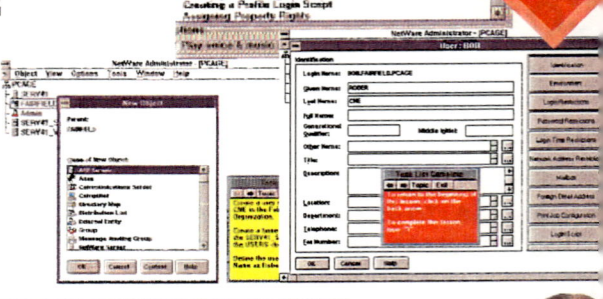

- Learn NetWare with step-by-step interactive training
- Practice NetWare utilities without installing NetWare
- Contains over 100 useful exercises and 60+ help screens for Server and Workstation
- NSEPro and MTL hands-on exercises
- Covers both NetWare 3.1x and IntranetWare 4.11

Do you need to study NetWare but don't want to jeopardize your current installation or don't have an installation at all? Whether you are studying for CNE exams or brushing up on your understanding of NetWare 3.1x or 4.11, the NetWare Interactive Simulator gives you hands-on experience with NetWare.

The NetWare Interactive Simulator contains over 100 NetWare 3.1x and 4.11 exercises; Its unique hands-on approach is useful for those complex Novell utilities that you just can't understand with books and study guides. With the NetWare Interactive Simulator, you learn NetWare by doing without harming your current NetWare installation or needing to be on a network at all!

No need for a File Server, Network Interface Cards (NICs), or NetWare

NetWare Interactive Simulator Item # NIS34-797 ...$2⁹
5 user version Item # 5NIS34-797 ......$9
10 user version Item # 10NIS34-797 ......$18
25+ user version, Call.
(shipped in CD-ROM only)

System Requirements: 486+ PC, Window 3.1+, 8 MB RAM, 2x CD-ROM Drive, 1-2 M hard disk space (as it runs from the CD-ROM)

Practice Taking the CNE Exams Right on Your PC

CNE TestMaster for Win/Win95/N

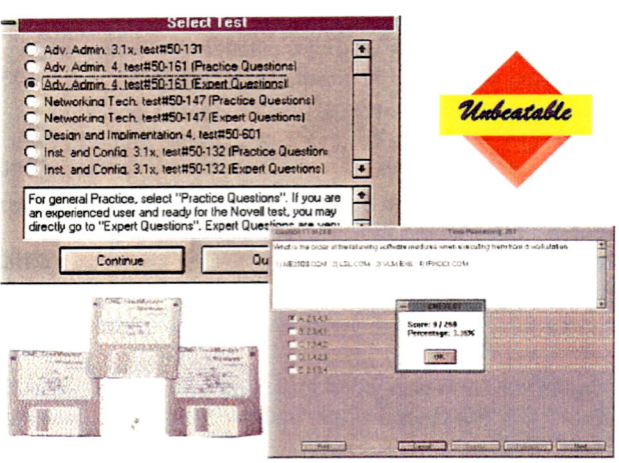

- Interactive software that simulates actual Novell tes
- More than 3000 multiple-choice practice questions
- Prepared by highly qualified and experienced instructo
- Covers both NetWare 3.1x and IntranetWare 4.11

You want to be a Certified Novell Engineer (CNE), b you are not sure whether you know the right NetWa details to pass the CNE exams. Now you can quiz yours and find out, right on your PC to determine your skills le before you take the exams.

CNE TestMaster Covers the Following Novell Tests:
Course 520, Administration 4.11
Course 525, Advanced Administration 4.11
Course 804, Installation & Configuration Workshop 4.11
Course 532, Design and Implementation 4.11
Course 540, Building Intranets with IntranetWare 4.11
Course 508, Administration 3.12
Course 518, Advanced Administration 3.12
Course 802, Installation & Configuration Workshop 3.12
Course 526, NetWare 3.1x to 4.11 Update
Course 801, Service & Support
Course 200, Networking Technologies
Course 605, NetWare TCP/IP Transport (elective)

CNE TestMaster, Item # CNETM34-797 ......$149
5 user version, Item # 5CNETM34-797 ......$595
10 user version Item # 10CNETM34-797 ......$995
25+ user version, Call.
(shipped in 3.5 inch disks only)

Note: Single test can be sold separately.

System Requirements: 386+ PC, Windows 3.1+, 4 MB RAM, 10 MB Hard Disk Space.

Order Today!!! 1-800-PCAGE-60 (1-800-722-4360)

PC Age, Inc.: 20 Audrey Place, Fairfield, NJ 07004. U.S.A. International: (01) 732-287-3622, Fax: (01) 732-287-45
Visit us on the WEB at: http://www.pcage.com or E-Mail: sales@pcage.com

Now You Can Practice Taking the MCSE Tests Right on Your PC

MCSE TestMaster™
for Win/Win95/NT

- Interactive software that simulates actual Microsoft tests
- Hundreds of multiple-choice practice questions and answers
- Checks your knowledge and highlights your areas of weakness
- Prepared by highly qualified and experienced instructors

You want to be a Microsoft Certified System Engineer (MCSE) or Microsoft Certified Product Specialist (MCPS), but you are not sure whether you know the right Windows NT details to pass MCSE or MCPS exam(s). Now you can quiz yourself and find out, determining your skills level right on your PC to before you take the test(s).

MCSE TestMaster helps you determine your skills level before you take the exam(s). It can save you the time, expense, aggravation, and embarrassment of failing an exam and having to study more to retake it.

MCSE TestMaster Any Single Test $139
MCSE TestMaster Core Pack (four tests) $495
MCSE TestMaster All Six Tests $695
For multi user version prices, call. (Shipped in 3.5 inch disks only)

System Requirements: 386+ PC, Windows 3.1+, 4 MB RAM, 10 MB of free Hard Disk space.

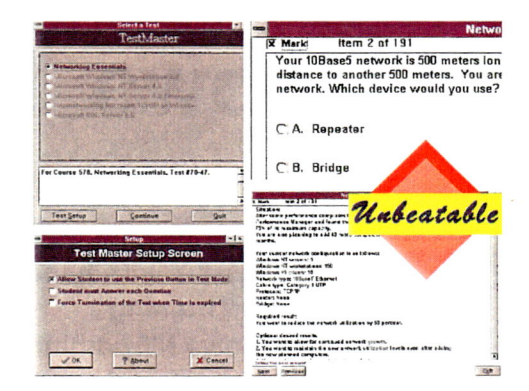

MCSE TestMaster Covers the Following Microsoft Tests

Core

Course 578, Networking Essentials, test #70-58

Course 687, Implementing and Supporting Microsoft Windows NT Workstation 4.0, test # 70-73

Course 687, Implementing and Supporting Microsoft Windows NT Server 4.0, test #70-67

Course 689, Implementing and Supporting Microsoft Windows NT Server 4.0 Enterprise Technologies, test #70-68

Electives

Course 688, Internetworking Microsoft TCP/IP on Windows NT, test #70-59

Course 867, System Administration for Microsoft SQL Server 6.5 for Windows NT, test #70-26

Guarantee to Pass Microsoft Tests:

PC Age offers you* a 90-Day 100% Money Back Guarantee. If you do not pass the Microsoft test(s) on two attempts within ninety (90) days of the purchase, call us and we will issue you a 100% credit for the MCSE TestMaster price. You do not need to return the TestMaster to us. It is yours to keep.

* This offer is good for the actual buyer only. Credit will be issued for the failed test(s) only (excluding shipping & handling). Proof of purchase may be required.

Order Today!!! 1-800-PCAGE-60 (1-800-722-4360)

PC Age, Inc.: 20 Audrey Place, Fairfield, NJ 07004. U.S.A. International: (01) 732-287-3622, Fax: (01) 732-287-4511
Visit us on the WEB at: http://www.pcage.com or E-Mail: sales@pcage.com

Effective 07/28/97

Learn Windows NT Administration with Hands On Interactive Exercises Without Having NT!

LearnByDoing™ Windows NT®

for Win/Win95/NT

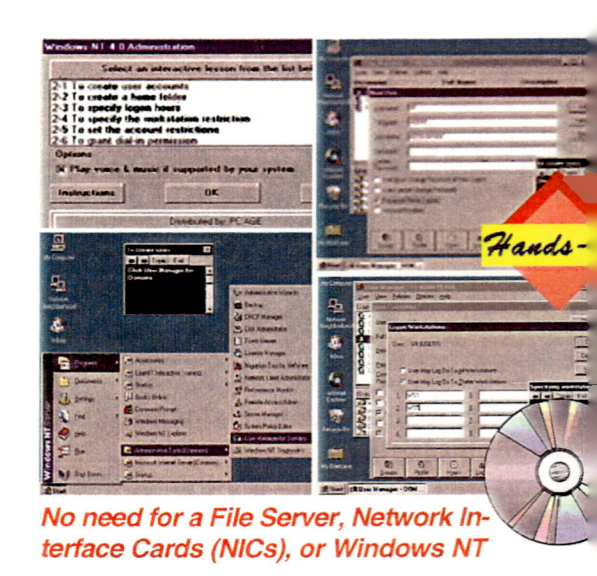

- Learn Windows NT with hands-on step-by-step interactive training
- Practice Windows NT administration without having to install NT or risk training on a running network
- Prepared by highly qualified and experienced instructors
- Helps you passing Microsoft MCSE/MCPS tests
- Compatible with all versions of Windows

No need for a File Server, Network Interface Cards (NICs), or Windows NT

Do you want to learn Windows NT Administration but don't want to jeopardize your current installation or don't have a Windows NT installation at all? Whether you are studying for Microsoft Certified Professional exams or brushing up on your understanding of Windows NT 4.0, the LearnByDoing Windows NT gives you hands-on experience with Windows NT.

LearnByDoing Windows NT Interactive Training contains hands-on interactive exercises to teach you administration of single user and single domain networks. Its unique hands-on approach is useful for those complex Windows NT utilities that you just can't understand with books and study guides. With the LearnByDoing Windows NT, you learn through actual practice without harming your current Windows NT installation or needing to be on a network at all!

Here is a listing of some of the hands-on interactive exercises covered in LearnByDoing Windows NT

- Creating user accounts
- Creating a home folder
- Specifying logon hours
- Specifying the workstation restriction
- Setting the account restrictions
- Granting dial-in permission
- Renaming a user account
- Deleting a user account
- Creating a template user profile
- Copying template user profile to a network server
- Specifying users who are permitted to use the profile
- Deleting the template profile user profile
- Creating a global group
- Adding members to a global group
- Determining the type of profile assigned to a user
- And many many more ...

LearnByDoing Windows NT 1 User Item No. LBDNT-797 ....$295
LearnByDoing Windows NT 5 User Item No. LBDNT5-797 ....$995
LearnByDoing Windows NT 10 User Item No. LBDNT10-797 ....$1895
25+ User, Call.
(Shipped in CD-ROM only)

System Requirements: 486+ PC, Windows 3.1+ MB-RAM, 2x CD-ROM Drive, 1-2 MB of free Hard Disk space

Order Today!!! 1-800-PCAGE-60 (1-800-722-4360)

PC Age, Inc.: 20 Audrey Place, Fairfield, NJ 07004. U.S.A. International: (01) 732-287-3622, Fax: (01) 732-287-451
Visit us on the WEB at: http://www.pcage.com or E-Mail: sales@pcage.com